STUDENT GUIDE
TO RESEARCH IN
THE DIGITAL AGE

STUDENT GUIDE
TO RESEARCH IN
THE DIGITAL AGE

How to Locate and Evaluate Information Sources

Leslie F. Stebbins

LIBRARIES

U N L I M I T E D

A Member of the Greenwood Publishing Group

Westport, Connecticut · London

Library of Congress Cataloging-in-Publication Data

Stebbins, Leslie F. (Leslie Foster)
    Student guide to research in the digital age : how to locate and evaluate
information sources / by Leslie F. Stebbins.
        p. cm.
    Includes bibliographical references and index.
    ISBN 1-59158-099-4 (pbk. : alk. paper)
    1. Research—Handbooks, manuals, etc.   2. Information retrieval—
Handbooks, manuals, etc.   3. Information resources—Evaluation—Handbooks,
manuals, etc.   4. Computer network resources—Handbooks, manuals, etc.
5. Electronic information resource searching—Handbooks, manuals, etc.
6. Library research—Handbooks, manuals, etc.   7. Bibliography—
Methodology—Handbooks, manuals, etc.   8. Report writing—Handbooks,
manuals, etc.   I. Title.
ZA3075.S74 2006
025.5'24—dc22   2005030844

British Library Cataloguing in Publication Data is available.

Library of Congress Catalog Card Number: 2005030844
ISBN: 1-59158-099-4

First published in 2006

Libraries Unlimited, 88 Post Road West, Westport, CT 06881
A Member of the Greenwood Publishing Group, Inc.
www.lu.com

Printed in the United States of America

The paper used in this book complies with the
Permanent Paper Standard issued by the National
Information Standards Organization (Z39.48–1984).

10 9 8 7 6 5 4 3

Everything should be made as simple as possible, but not simpler.
—Albert Einstein

Contents

Preface

A friend of mine who has dangerously high cholesterol levels and is taking six medications recently visited a nutritionist to look into alternative ways of reducing his cholesterol. The nutritionist advised my friend to become a vegetarian immediately, exercise an hour a day, meditate, take up yoga, and eliminate caffeine and sugar from his diet. Overwhelmed with this advice, he immediately proceeded to the grocery store where he purchased two cartons of Häagen-Dazs ice cream.

In some ways a research project can resemble my friend's trip to the nutritionist—so overwhelming that there is a temptation to fall back on a Google search, grab a few items, and begin writing. Unfortunately, using a massive search engine like Google will not provide you with the most scholarly, relevant, and reliable resources on your topic. A research paper is only as good as the quality of the resources upon which it is based.

This book is essential reading for any student embarking on a research assignment. The most challenging aspect of research today is finding *too much* on a topic and having to choose which information resources are the most important to include in your paper. *Student Guide to Research in the Digital Age: How to Locate and Evaluate Information Sources* is designed to teach students how to find and evaluate scholarly resources on the web and in print.

Each chapter of this book discusses when to use a particular type of resource, how to find it, and how to evaluate it. Critical evaluation is presented as a component of every stage of research from formulating a research question, choosing tools to search, developing search strategies, and selecting resources. The web is presented as both a complex medium which distributes scholarly electronic journals, ebooks, digitized primary source collections, and other rich scholarly resources, as well as a provider of massive amounts of more limited and potentially unreliable information that needs to be used cautiously, if at all.

Evaluation skills are introduced as both a set of concrete techniques that can be applied to a particular type of information, as well as a more creative and intuitive process that is developed over time as knowledge about a subject grows. This book promotes using filters, such as specialized databases and tools, to focus the research process and weed out extraneous and less scholarly information. Students are encouraged to recognize contextual clues to gain meaning and provide evaluative criteria for choosing appropriate information resources; at the same time they are advised to examine their own assumptions about a topic and be willing to adjust their own ideas based on previous research. In addition, the authority of a source, its purpose and scholarly nature, and issues of accuracy, currency, and relevance are explored.

Unlike the advice of the nutritionist above, this book is *not* meant to be digested in one sitting. The comprehensive table of contents and extensive index can be used to focus on an immediate need.

Chapter 1 serves as an introduction to research and critical evaluation. It provides a step-by-step process that novice as well as more advanced students can follow for any research assignment:

1. Define your research question
2. Ask for help
3. Develop a research strategy and locate resources
4. Use effective search techniques
5. Read critically, synthesize, and seek meaning
6. Understand the scholarly communication process and cite sources
7. Critically evaluate sources

Chapters 2 through 7 focus on specific types of information resources. Recognizing when to use a particular type of resource, understanding how the information is organized, choosing appropriate search tools, and developing evaluation strategies specific to certain types of resources is discussed in these chapters.

- Books (chapter 2)
- Articles (chapter 3)
- Primary sources (chapter 4)
- Biographical resources (chapter 5)
- Legal resources (chapter 6)
- Government documents and statistics (chapter 7)

Chapter 8 focuses on how to develop a system for taking notes, when to paraphrase or use direct quotes, how to properly cite a source and avoid plagiarism, how to use specialized software to format your footnotes or endnotes, and how to bring critical evaluation techniques into the process.

Unlike earlier books on library research, this book emphasizes critical evaluation as an ever-present component of the research process. This book moves beyond basic computer and search skills that in the days of Google and IM are second nature to "millennial" students. Instead the focus is on recognizing what types of information resources are needed, how to select the most appropriate tools and search strategies for the information needed, and how to apply evaluation strategies that are specific to the type of information being explored.

Finally, this book strives to provide a conceptual understanding of research as an ongoing scholarly conversation that the student is entering. Research does not occur in a vacuum, but is a process in which the boundaries of knowledge are gradually pushed forward while staying tethered to what has already been uncovered.

Acknowledgments

Every book is a collaborative work, and many advisors, friends, and family have assisted in the production of this one. I would especially like to thank librarians and good friends Sue Woodson and Sally Wyman; Brandeis professors Janet Giele, Jytte Klausen, and Karen Hansen; and my reader of first resort, husband, and former librarian, Tom Blumenthal. Thanks also to my editors Martin Dillon and Sue Easun and the staff at Libraries Unlimited. And thanks also to the following librarians who let me tap into their expertise in a variety of areas: Judy Pinnolis, Laura Reiner, Kelsey Libner, Susan Pyzynski, and Ralph Szymczak. Also, a big thank you to the undergraduates at Brandeis University who have taught me so much about student research. And, as always, thanks to Anna and Will for their support and patience.

1

Research and Critical Evaluation

There is no way of exchanging information that does not demand an act of judgment.

Jacob Bronowski

Research and critical evaluation strategies are the most important skills you will learn in college. Whatever field or hobby you pursue there will be a need to effectively collect, analyze, and evaluate information. Information literacy skills are powerful, even radical abilities that allow anyone to pursue knowledge in any field or on any subject. Unfortunately, these skills are largely self-taught and haphazardly developed.

There is no one right way to do research, though the stages of research listed below are part of most research endeavors. Similarly, evaluation skills developed initially as a set of concrete techniques come to more closely resemble a creative and intuitive act. Everyone does research and critical evaluation differently, and even experienced scholars will research a subject in their field of study differently from a topic that is outside their area of expertise.

So how do you do research? Beginning researchers need to start by using the seven steps listed below. The path is not always linear, but these steps provide a framework for conducting research. Many beginning researchers leave out the critical evaluation component of research. When confronted with a number of search tools, they use the one they are most familiar with instead of the best tool for their topic; when confronted with a list of resources, they choose the first three instead of analyzing and selecting the most important, reputable, and relevant titles.

The most challenging aspect of research today is finding *too much* information on a topic. The ability to critically evaluate tools and resources cannot be developed in twenty minutes; it is a lifelong developmental process. Critical evaluation involves asking questions and consciously making choices. Evaluation skills will ultimately make the difference between an adequate research paper and an excellent one.

This chapter walks you through the seven steps of research:

1. Define your research question
2. Ask for help
3. Develop a research strategy and locate resources
4. Use effective search techniques
5. Read critically, synthesize, and seek meaning
6. Understand the scholarly communication process and cite sources
7. Critically evaluate sources

Chapters 2 through 7 of this book focus on finding and evaluating specific types of resources: books (chapter 2); journal, magazine, and newspaper articles (chapter 3); primary sources (chapter 4); biographical resources (chapter 5); legal resources (chapter 6); government documents and statistics (chapter 7). The final chapter covers the subjects of organizing research, taking notes, avoiding plagiarism, and citing sources.

FOLLOW THE SEVEN STEPS OF RESEARCH, BUT BE FLEXIBLE!

The seven steps are presented here in a logical order, but they are not always followed in a linear way from step one to step two and so on. Research frequently involves jumping back and forth between stages. A researcher might develop a hypothesis, retrieve and read a few initial articles or books, then go back and revise the hypothesis, and then start out again in a slightly different direction. Keep an open mind as you go through the research steps outlined below, be willing to jump back and forth between steps, and be open minded about the direction your own research might take. Research involves a combination of using the work of scholars that have gone before you, while at the same time taking small steps onto new terrain.

STEP ONE: DEFINE YOUR RESEARCH QUESTION

Topic refinement is an ongoing activity as you go through the research process. A vague idea about a subject area gradually turns into a topic, aspects of the topic are evaluated, and a research question or hypothesis is developed. Finally, when writing the paper, a thesis statement is articulated.

A **topic** is a general subject area such as global warming or after-school child care. Choosing a research topic is challenging. It is a process, not just something you sit and think about. It is important to devote time to choosing a topic, but do not get so bogged down that you spend a large percentage of the time you have allotted to doing research on defining the topic. Think concretely about your topic and do a few sample searches in article databases (see chapter 3) to see how other researchers have approached your topic. A topic needs to have intellectual energy—it needs to be interesting to other scholars and fit into the larger current research landscape. You are breaking into a scholarly conversation that is already going on, and your remarks need to be relevant to what is currently under study. The topic should:

- interest you enough that you are willing to spend hours learning more about it,
- be complex and multifaceted,
- generate one or more research questions relating to it,
- have generated some research by other scholars,
- be broad enough that you can find materials, but narrow enough for you to explore in a research paper.

The subject of racism would be too broad, but racism in American schools in the 1950s might be narrow enough to pursue in a ten-page paper. On the other hand, senior citizens who find pleasure listening to garage music is probably too narrow a topic, with little if any scholarly research available. A quick article database search should turn up at least a few articles related to your topic. A search that turns up hundreds of articles is an indication that your topic is too broad. Limiting the search to a geographic area or specific time period, or investigating only one aspect of a multifaceted topic can help narrow search results.

Your **hypothesis** is an educated guess, a prediction, asked in the form of a question. Your hypothesis attempts to predict your thesis.

Does deforestation contribute to global warming?
Does the existence of after-school programs for inner-city middle school students reduce juvenile drug use?

After you have chosen a general topic, do some brief initial research. Read a newspaper or encyclopedia article or skim through the introduction of a book on your topic. What are the common questions or themes that relate to your topic? What is controversial about your topic? What have researchers pursued in relation to your topic? Your hypothesis should be adjusted over time as you uncover research supporting or contradicting your ideas. If your hypothesis was that deforestation has a significant impact on global warming but all the research indicates the opposite, you might want to modify your hypothesis or even change your hypothesis to focus on some other causal agent of global warming. Research is not the same as preparing for a debate. Research involves looking into what is out there and being prepared for some surprises.

A **thesis** is what you will develop toward the end of your research, after you have read and analyzed the research on a topic. The thesis is a general statement in your paper that presents your conclusions. Your paper then provides the support for the conclusion stated in your thesis. A thesis might be: Quality after-school programs greatly reduce teenage drug use, but poorly managed or underfunded programs have little impact on teenage drug use.

A great deal of work and critical evaluation goes into refining your topic and developing your hypothesis and thesis. This work is what is taking place as you carry out the research process. As you gather, read, analyze, and take notes on information about your subject, continue to revisit your hypothesis and adjust it as needed based on the information you are gathering. Once you have clearly articulated your research question (hypothesis), the thesis is an answer to the question.

Have flu shots proven to be effective for certain populations?
becomes the thesis statement:
Flu shots have been proven to be effective for children and the elderly.

STEP TWO: ASK FOR HELP

Many students are reluctant to ask for assistance with a research assignment. They feel they should already know how to do research, that research is not that difficult, and that asking for help from a professor, teaching assistant, or librarian will in some way lessen their credibility. Students who do not ask for help pay a high price in misunderstood assignments and poorly conducted research. Teaching faculty, instructors, and librarians can provide assistance in the research process. Asking for help makes the teaching and learning process successful.

Ask an instructor for help defining or selecting a topic, understanding the research paper assignment, or identifying some of the key books or articles on a topic. One of the greatest evaluative resources you have access to is your professors—use them. Faculty members have large internal "knowledge banks" that enable them to look at a long list of resources about a topic and identify the more valuable titles through familiarity and experience with particular authors, scholarly journals, publishers, and so on.

Librarians can provide help with almost all aspects of the research process other than clarification of an assignment and topic selection. In particular, librarians can assist in designing search strategies and critically evaluating the flood of information on your topic, but they can lack in-depth expertise on a specific topic. In working with a librarian, it is up to you to be as clear as possible about the research area you are pursuing and the research questions you want answered.

STEP THREE: DEVELOP A RESEARCH STRATEGY AND LOCATE RESOURCES

Developing an effective research strategy involves deciding what types of resources are needed (e.g., books, journal articles, government documents) and what tools (e.g., library online catalogs, journal databases) will enable you to access resources on your topic.

Find Books

Many research papers longer than a few pages require a review of books that have been written related to your research question. Monographs, scholarly books focusing on one topic in a thorough manner, can be useful because they provide a broad, as well as deep, overview of a topic. While journal and magazine articles often focus on one narrowly defined aspect of an issue, books provide the background and analysis of a subject and place the research question in a larger context.

Often the first step in a research project is to review subject encyclopedia articles about the topic under study. More and more specialized encyclopedias are now found in ebook form. Details about locating background information in books in print and online, strategies for locating books generally, and techniques for critically evaluating books can be found in chapter 2.

Find Journal, Magazine, and Newspaper Articles

Most research involves a review of the current scholarly writing about a subject. Scholarly journal articles contain the findings of research being conducted in all disciplines and areas. Today there are more than 10,000 scholarly journals, many available online, that cover every area imaginable. For each research area (e.g., Latin American literature, child development) there are usually a dozen or more respected journals devoted to publishing articles by faculty members and other scholars. Though journal articles often focus on a narrow aspect of a subject, topics are usually similar in scope to that of a ten- or twenty-page research paper. The crucial factor to remember in locating journal articles is that most are not free and can best be located by searching library databases that will provide you with institutional access to these articles. Choosing the right databases to search is imperative.

Researchers rely less on newspapers and magazines because although these sources may be factually accurate, they are written by journalists who are typically generalists rather than experts (for example, a journalist who covers health issues for a local newspaper). Unlike authors of scholarly journal articles who are specialists with expertise in a specific area, journalists cover topics more superficially—they are reporting on recent research or news events. Though many student research papers contain citations to newspaper and magazine articles, these sources should be balanced with research from more weighty research journals. Chapter 3 provides information on how to select journal, magazine, and newspaper databases and techniques for critically evaluating these resources.

Find Specialized Resources

Specialized resources include any information resource that is *not* a book, journal, magazine, or current newspaper article. They include:

- primary source materials such as historical newspapers, archival materials, and manuscripts (chapter 4)
- biographical resources such as letters, diaries, or oral histories (chapter 5)
- case law and specialized legal resources (chapter 6)
- government documents and statistics (chapter 7)

Historical research and projects that require analysis of primary sources are more likely to include specialized resources. These resources are rewarding to work with—in some cases you may be one of the first people to view a document or pull disparate items together to analyze a historical subject in a new way. Locating and evaluating these resources can be challenging. Specific tools and evaluative criteria are discussed in chapters 4 through 7.

Find Web Resources

There are two types of resources available on the web. The first type is published vetted resources that use the web as a medium for information delivery, such as the *Journal of American History*. The second type consists of web pages that are self-published and do not go through any type of quality control process such as a student blog or homepage. Many professors warn their students against relying on the web for research. They are referring to the unpublished unfiltered web rather than published resources that use the web as an information delivery mechanism.

Though scholars differ on the definition of what is "published," a published resource (whether on the web or in print) has generally undergone some type of vetting process including editing, fact-checking, or peer review, making it a more reliable resource. Peer review involves experts in a field reviewing and providing feedback on the work of other scholars before the publishing process is completed. The publisher provides a stamp of approval by standing behind and being associated with a particular work. For example, the American Medical Association vouches for the validity of articles published in its *Journal of the American Medical Association.*

Researchers rely largely on published sources, either online or in print, that have undergone some type of review by reputable institutions. Web pages—unpublished materials located on the web—should only be used as a last resort or when particularly relevant to the topic under study. There are times when relying on web pages is necessary for some types of research, but it is important that the majority of resources used and included in the bibliography of a research paper be published or vetted in some way, regardless of format. There are times when web pages can themselves be primary documents that are analyzed for research purposes; this is quite different from citing these pages as authoritative support for your thesis.

STEP FOUR: USE EFFECTIVE SEARCH TECHNIQUES

Once you have decided what types of resources you will pursue and which databases are most appropriate for searching for those resources (consulting chapters 2 through 7), the next step is to learn efficient search techniques. These techniques involve understanding the content of a particular tool or database and knowing how to devise a search statement that will be precise enough to capture what you want, while not being so restrictive that it fails to retrieve important titles.

Many library databases, such as online library catalogs and journal and magazine databases, have similar characteristics. Boolean searching, keyword and subject heading searching, and other tricks such as limit setting, truncation, and proximity searching can enhance research efficiency.

Use Boolean Searching to Combine Concepts and Search Synonyms

Boolean searching (using "and," "or," "not") should be used to broaden and narrow search results. For example, for research on French advertisements, do not just search:

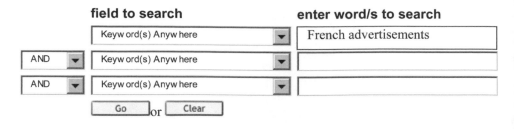

Instead, join concepts using "and," and search synonyms using "or":

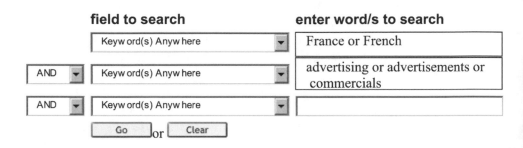

Use "or" to denote that any, but not necessarily all, of the words connected by "or" need to be retrieved. Use "and" to denote that at least one item from the first search set and one item from the second search set need to be retrieved. Boolean searching is essential for retrieving all the items on your topic. If you are searching for articles on drug abuse but most researchers are calling it "substance abuse," failing to use synonyms will result in missing most of the records in a database.

Use "not" with caution because sometimes it can eliminate useful results. "Not" can be invaluable when searching for such things as the country Turkey:

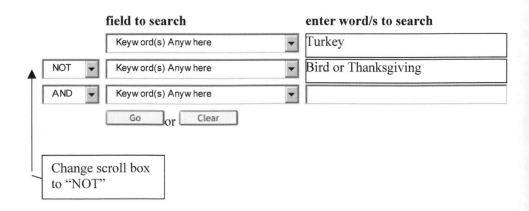

Use Keyword Searching

Keyword or "free text" searching, the default setting in most databases, involves searching most of the text in each record in the database. A record contains information about each work, such as author, title, publisher, description, and subject. When doing keyword searching, include synonyms for every concept. For example, if you are searching for books or articles on domestic violence, the search "family violence" might turn up a few, but not all the titles on this subject. Instead, break your research question into concepts—in this case "family" and "violence." Then develop synonyms for each concept:

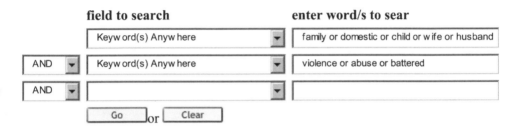

field to search	enter word/s to sear
Keyword(s) Anywhere ▼	family or domestic or child or wife or husband
AND ▼ Keyword(s) Anywhere ▼	violence or abuse or battered
AND ▼ ▼	

Go   or   Clear

Use Subject Heading or Descriptor Searching

Most databases are "subject indexed," meaning each title has been reviewed and assigned several subject descriptors based on its content. This provides a powerful opportunity for searching *if* the special subject headings are known. Most academic library online catalogs use the same system—Library of Congress Subject Headings—but many journal, magazine, or other resource databases use their own specialized vocabulary.

The best way to conduct "controlled vocabulary" (subject heading) searching is to start with a keyword search using synonyms (described directly above). Once you have retrieved some results, choose a few titles that most accurately reflect your topic. Then look at each full record to uncover what subject headings or descriptors were used to index that title. Go back to the search screen and enter one of those subject headings. This usually involves changing a pull-down box to "subject" or "descriptor." Subject heading searching retrieves more precise results and is useful when keyword searching is bringing up too many irrelevant results. The complete database of Library of Congress Subject Headings is available at http://authorities.loc.gov/.

Use Other Tricks to Narrow Search Results

Most databases provide techniques for reducing the number of titles retrieved. These techniques are described by clicking the "Help" button in any database or online catalog.

Limit setting involves narrowing results, usually by checking off boxes or making selections on scroll boxes. Limits can be set for publishing date, language, availability, or type of resource retrieved. Sometimes the "advanced" search option needs to be selected to employ limits.

Limit search to:

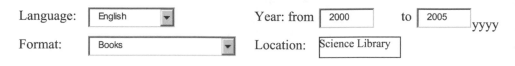

Truncation involves using a symbol to catch all possible endings of a word. For example both "advertising" and "advertisement" can be retrieved by searching "advertis*." Truncation symbols are typically an asterisk or a question mark. Symbols used by a specific catalog or database are indicated in the help screens.

Proximity searching or phrase searching is employed using a variety of symbols also indicated in the database help files. Some databases put quotation marks around a phrase to indicate a phrase search. Others use "w" for "with" or "n" for "near" so that the phrase "global warming" is indicated as: "global w1 warming." This means "global" within one word of "warming," a more precise search that will not pick up irrelevant records that mention "global" in the title and the word "warming" related to some other context later in the record.

STEP FIVE: READ CRITICALLY, SYNTHESIZE, AND SEEK MEANING

Critical reading involves actively engaging with the text before, during, and after you read it. This can be a new experience for many students who are used to taking most published resources at face value. Question and challenge everything you read to see if it "passes muster." Decide what is worthy of incorporating into your own research and what needs to be discarded, based *not* on whether ideas match your own, but on careful analysis of the veracity of the researcher's work.

- Begin by quickly scanning the pages you will be reading. Observe the structure, skim the abstract, read the headings, and note the author credentials if indicated. Observe the level of the text and think about what the author is trying to accomplish or prove.
- Next, take notes about key points in the text, make note of your own reactions to these ideas, and add any questions or additional ideas you might

have about what the text is discussing. Try to tease out the main points and key arguments and put together an outline or concise summary of the writing—*in your own words*. Indicate what the author is relying on to prove the assertions made in the text. Keep your notes organized and concise.

- Lastly, put the writing in context and analyze it. Compare it with your own ideas and what others have written on the topic. What evidence does this author give to support a particular claim? How does this author's writing impact your own views?

Be prepared to feel overwhelmed and confused! The beginning stages of reading and taking notes involve a great deal of uncertainty. If done correctly, there is an ongoing process of formulating tentative hypotheses, reading and analyzing information, and then adjusting the hypotheses or even the entire topic accordingly. Research sometimes involves being hit in the face with valid research that contradicts or at the least shifts your current thinking on a subject. One piece of research can also disagree with another piece of research, and further information and analysis needs to take place. Research can be uncomfortable as well as exciting!

As you gather more information, you will begin to develop a thread or a series of patterns that start to fit together. As this occurs, the comfort level rises and the research area becomes more focused, interesting, and manageable (Grassian and Kaplowitz 2001).

Esther Grassian and Joan Kaplowitz (2001) suggest organizing your thoughts about a research question by keeping a research log or journal and spending ten minutes every day:

- clarifying or redefining your topic or research area
- noting important discoveries you have made relating to your topic
- indicating what questions you still need answered

Frequently reviewing what you have learned, as well as what you have left to do, makes it easier to return to your research process the following day.

STEP SIX: UNDERSTAND THE SCHOLARLY COMMUNICATION PROCESS AND CITE SOURCES

When you pick up a scholarly book or article, you enter into a conversation taking place around a particular topic among a group of experts. For any topic—chaos theory, child abuse, Shakespeare—there is a group of academicians who are participating in an ongoing dialogue that pushes the boundaries of our understanding of that topic. By picking up a scholarly book or article, you are entering into a conversation that may have started some time ago and that probably continues past the publication date of the title you are reading. The participants are connected to the others by recording their research via the writing of a book or journal article. By citing previous research on the topic, a scholar ties his or her own research into the conversation.

Research involves pulling together the strands of the conversation that relate to the topic you are interested in pursuing, and building upon all that is currently known about that area. Knowledge does not exist in a vacuum. Knowledge-building is an ongoing, interconnected process, and research involves tapping into the grapevine of scholarly debate about a topic and making sure you uncover all the key contributing voices. When you have reached this point, you can begin to contribute potential building blocks of your own.

When Stephen Hawking wrote *A Brief History of Time* in 1988, it was a widely acclaimed scholarly book for which he received great applause. However, like any scholarly book, it was not a solo endeavor. That is not to say that Hawking plagiarized from others, but he did what any reputable scholar does—he entered the scholarly conversation on quantum mechanics, and building on previous research, he presented additional building blocks that he piled on top of the earlier research. More than a decade later, additional blocks have been added to what we know about quantum mechanics and some of Hawking's ideas have been disproved.

As you do your research, you will tie your ideas into the work that has gone on before you. Keep an open mind as you get up to speed on the current research about a topic. As you are gathering your resources together, develop an organized system of note-taking and keeping track of citations that will later be needed for your bibliography. Systems for organizing your research, taking notes, avoiding plagiarism, using a style manual, and making use of bibliographic software are explained in chapter 8.

Making the decision that your research is complete and that it is time to write your paper depends on the size of the paper you are writing and the degree to which you are expected to cover a topic. A two- or three-page research paper might require only a few titles to be included in the bibliography, but choosing that key handful can involve reviewing and discarding many others. For longer assignments, such as a senior honors thesis or dissertation, there is a gratifying sense of coming full circle. After searching several major library catalogs and journal databases relating to a topic and tracing relevant sources listed in the bibliographies of these articles and books, the researcher begins to see the same authors and titles repeatedly. It is at this point that the researcher knows a comprehensive literature search has been accomplished. Not an easy feat in the "information age."

STEP SEVEN: CRITICALLY EVALUATE SOURCES

Critical evaluation involves using analytical thinking skills within the context of conducting research. Critical evaluation is an active process that comes into play at every stage of the research process—during topic selection; choosing databases to search; selecting books, articles, and other sources to read; and choosing which resources will ultimately be used and cited in the research paper. Though each stage is important, the final stage of choosing which resources to include in your paper is where critical evaluation skills need to be the most actively engaged.

Critical evaluation ranges from a series of mechanical techniques and strategies that can be applied to almost any information resource to the more abstract and intuitive activities involved in using your own "knowledge bank"—the knowledge you are gradually acquiring about a topic—to evaluate new information resources. As your own knowledge bank grows you will be able to more extensively evaluate resources that you uncover.

Initial mechanical techniques might involve questions such as "How recently was this book written?" or "Is this a scholarly source?" Deeper evaluative questions will relate to the content of the material and how it compares to earlier research. A researcher using these deeper critical evaluation skills is able to contribute in a meaningful way to the scholarly conversation that is taking place about a specific research area. By tying into prior research in a critical and significant way, a scholar is then able to add new building blocks to the work of earlier scholars.

The following strategies are generic in that they can be applied to almost any resource. They should become second nature to you as you gain experience as a researcher. The chapters that follow present additional strategies that can be used with specific types of resources.

Use Filters

Filters are something we use as we go through everyday life. We shop at a particular shoe store because we know the quality or style of shoes will be better; we see a particular movie based on the recommendation of a trusted friend; we buy coffee at one cafe and not another because we are familiar with the quality of the brand. Using filters saves time and improves the chances of getting higher quality goods.

When doing research there are many opportunities to use filters.

- Using an academic library online catalog rather than Amazon.com limits your search results to scholarly books that have been screened and purchased by librarians.

- Using a database that covers scholarly journal articles screens out any un-published writings that have not been edited or fact-checked.
- Using an article found in a scholarly journal provides an intense filtering process. A paper must be accepted by a journal editor and undergo peer review, editing, and fact-checking.
- Using bibliographies listed at the back of scholarly books, journal articles, or subject encyclopedias provides access to relevant quality titles. These authors have provided authoritative screening for you by selecting what they felt were the most important articles. A great deal of scholarly research is conducted by tracing the bibliographies of other researchers.
- Asking for recommendations from professors or other experts can help you focus on key articles on a topic. Their years of knowledge and extensive reading provide a valuable human filter that can point to key resources.
- Using the *Web of Science,* a database that traces which journal articles are heavily cited by other researchers, can lead you to articles that might carry more weight within a community of scholars. New databases *Scopus* and *Google Scholar* provide similar though less comprehensive services.

Many expert researchers use the phenomenon known as the "invisible college" as a filtering device. The "invisible college" is a loosely defined network of scholars, all working on similar research questions, who become familiar to each other through work, conference attendance, shared research interests, and publications. The internet has made the "invisible college" more accessible to student researchers by sometimes opening up listservs, blogs, discussion boards, and conference proceedings to anyone who is interested. Through interactions with this network, key works, authors, and important journals can be uncovered.

Use Context to Decipher Meaning and Evaluate

In *The Social Life of Information,* Brown and Daguid (2000) discuss the role of context in finding meaning in information. They give the example of listening to a lecture. The lecture is more than the text of the words that are delivered. Listeners use the setting, the speaker's clothing, presentation style, accent, emphasis, and background to enhance their understanding and evaluation of the content of the talk.

Similarly, many books and journal articles include contextual clues such as publisher information, the quality of the binding and paper, and the presence of advertising or pictures, that are useful for evaluation and understanding. Some web sites provide few contextual clues that can inform an evaluation. On the other hand, even the presentation of a web site can provide evidence about its content. If the web site contains advertising or has spelling or formatting errors, this indicates a lack of attention to detail and possibly a lack of accuracy. A web site that appears accurate is not guaranteed to be accurate, but a web site that exhibits questionable advertising, poorly worded sentences, or spelling mistakes indicates that the content may also be poorly constructed.

Using context to make informed decisions about what information to use for your research and what to discard can only partially be taught. It is a matter of life experience, common sense, and knowledge. Just as you know that a television commercial advertising a cure for baldness is suspect, and that a reputable newscaster's report of a possible cure for baldness might have some validity, experience and knowledge provide you with the ability to weigh contextual information and make choices. As a beginning researcher working within a particular discipline, some contextual clues might be less apparent to you. As you further your studies in a particular field, you will be able to recognize clues, such as the names and reputations of particular authors or journals, which will allow you to make more informed decisions.

Examine Your Assumptions

As a researcher, one of the most difficult things to let go of are your own assumptions. The reason you were motivated to research a particular subject in the first place is often related to your personal views or beliefs. You do not have to abandon your personal value system to conduct research, but it is important to acknowledge and set aside your personal beliefs while you are gathering information on your topic. As you pull together resources, be open to changing or adjusting your own set of beliefs about a particular topic.

For example, if you set off to prove that gun control will reduce the murder rate, you must investigate the past research that has been conducted on this topic, including those articles that may disagree with your thesis. Evaluate these articles for their merits and include those that have viable contributions to make. Rather than ignore, you must consider and address the research that might disagree with your hypothesis.

Evaluate Authority

Evaluating authority means investigating the credentials of both the author and the publisher or sponsor of the information resource. What are the author's credentials? In a book or journal article, a brief biography is sometimes available at the beginning or end. Check on what institutions the author is affiliated with and the author's areas of expertise. Has the author published other works on this subject? Do other authors cite this author in their works? It is also essential to examine the assumptions and motivations of other researchers. Every author you read should be evaluated carefully for hidden or even subconscious bias, faulty logic, or poorly designed research strategies. Differentiate between fact and opinion.

If the resource is published, who is the publisher? Is the publisher a university press, a commercial publisher, a nonprofit organization, or a government agency? Is the publisher affiliated with a religious or political organization? Some possible bias might be uncovered if the resource is tied to an organization that has a specific purpose for putting out information about a topic.

If a resource such as a brochure or a web page is not published, sometimes additional detective work must be conducted. Discovering the author's credentials might involve checking book or journal databases to see if the author has published books or articles that might indicate the author's experience. Figuring out what institution is serving a web page can also give further clues as to its reliability, but note whether the page is a personal one sitting on an institutional server or if the page is authorized by that institution. For example, a report of recent research might be part of an official Yale University web page, while a Yale student's personal page is not an officially sanctioned source even though it has a Yale web address.

Determine Purpose and Scholarly Nature

Try to uncover the purpose of a particular resource. What is the goal of the book, article, or web site? Was it written to present research findings and further knowledge, or is it more of an attempt to persuade, inform, or put forward an opinion? Who is the intended audience? Was the piece written for a scholarly group of researchers or specialists, an educated layperson, or does the language and message seem to be intended for the general public? Does the source seem to have a particular bias? Is the source scholarly?

A scholarly source can be spotted by:

- the level and tone of the language,
- the length—it is rare to see a two-page scholarly article,
- an extensive bibliography of reputable sources,
- an indication that research was conducted and conclusions were drawn, rather than a simple reporting of events,
- an author who is a professor or other expert in the field,
- little, if any, advertising present,
- an indication that a scholarly press, scholarly society, or academic institute published it,
- respected researchers making reference to it in their bibliographies.

Investigate Accuracy

Does the content seem accurate? Is the language informal or scholarly? Does it make sense? Does the writing seem to push for a particular agenda? Are there misspellings or is faulty logic used? Are statements backed up by citations to other scholarly research, or do they seem to be opinions of the author?

Try to locate a review or evaluation of the work in question. What do others think about what this author is asserting? How does it compare to other research on the subject? Does the bibliography provide a list of scholarly research on the subject? Is the work published? Was an editor, fact-checker, or some other vetting process employed before this information was made public?

Consider the plausibility of the information being presented. Check for external consistency. If information is being presented that is contrary to everything you know about a topic, the information should be regarded with some suspicion. Check also for internal consistency. Are the arguments that are being made supported within the work itself?

Note Currency

For some research the currency of a particular book or article is essential. In some sciences, such as molecular biology or genetics, research in a book more than a year old is long out of date and cannot be relied on for accurate information. In the humanities, sometimes older, more reputable studies can carry a great deal of weight and are important to cite in your research. For many social science topics, a source a few years old is considered relevant, but a descriptive or statistical resource more than ten years old is often considered too out of date to be useful. However, classic works relating to theory continue to be useful for a much longer period of time in the social sciences.

Determine Relevance

This may seem obvious, but the sources you use need to be relevant to the topic you are investigating. It is often tempting to include information that is interesting or exciting, but it may not further the goals of your research paper. When collecting resources to use for your paper, compare each source to the other sources you have gathered. Does one particular source add anything to the research you are presenting? What is the relative value of the source in question? Also be careful not to take other research and bend it to fit your hypothesis.

Use Higher-Order Thinking Skills to Select Resources

Critical evaluation involves using mechanistic steps as well as bringing in higher-order thinking skills at every stage of the research process. From formulating and reformulating your hypothesis as your work progresses to choosing which resources to cite in your final product, critical evaluation, the act of investigating the "worth, accuracy or authenticity of various propositions, leading to a supportable decision or direction for action" (Jones 1996) is an ongoing challenge.

Many of these higher-order skills are intuitive and develop over time as the researcher gains experience. They cannot be taught in a systematic way. Ultimately they involve building a large internal knowledge bank about the topic under study and tapping into this expertise. This also involves becoming familiar with the methodologies, techniques, and strategies within a particular discipline or field. For a short undergraduate research paper this is not possible, but for a senior honors thesis or graduate-level paper it is vital.

Scholars such as psychologists or biologists incorporate these higher-order skills as a matter of course. The longer you spend embedded within a particular discipline, the greater your experience will become in recognizing sound research designs, reputable and trustworthy research, and the plausibility of particular results.

Evaluation of information resources is an interpretive art as well as a science. It is based on sound ideas, experience, practice, creativity, and knowledge as well as other learned strategies and techniques. It is a lifelong developmental process. Sifting through information on a topic and deciding what is important and what is not helps us synthesize information and construct our own understanding and interpretation. By creating new knowledge, resting on the shoulders of earlier attempts, we add our voice to the scholarly conversation.

Be Engaged

Knowledge cannot be gained in a passive way. Active participation is required during the research process. A critical engaged spirit is needed in order to evaluate information and think critically about your own thought processes as you select and discard information resources to use for your research. Develop a questioning approach to everything you discover. This is different from criticizing everything you discover. Critically evaluating information means actively searching for the truth.

Recognize the gaps in your own knowledge. Being aware of what you do *not* know will guide you in your research. Keep a journal or notes to:

- record your thought processes and research strategies,
- argue with yourself,
- jot down creative ideas to pursue,
- list questions to be answered,
- explore different trains of thought,
- speculate and make predictions,
- discern patterns and meaning in information,
- apply what you know to new information you discover.

Much of this writing will not find its way into the final product, but the ideas explored will improve the end result.

Be open to serendipitous discoveries. The research process is an act of learning as well as a way to make a contribution. It is a collaborative process that ties into an ongoing conversation that is pushing the boundaries of what is known.

REFERENCES

Bronowski, Jacob. 1974. *The ascent of man.* Boston: Little, Brown.

Brown, John Seely, and Paul Daguid. 2000. *The social life of information.* Boston: Harvard Business School Press.

Grassian, Esther, and Joan Kaplowitz. 2001. *Information literacy instruction: Theory and practice.* New York: Neal-Schuman.

Jones, Debra. 1996. Critical thinking in an online world. *Untangling the Web, Proceedings of the Conference Sponsored by the Librarians Association of the University of California, Santa Barbara and Friends of the UCSB Library,* 26 April. http://www.library.ucsb.edu/untangle/jones.html. Accessed March 8, 2005.

2

Finding Books and Ebooks

Some books are to be tasted, others to be swallowed, and some few to be chewed and digested.

Francis Bacon

BOOKS AND SCHOLARLY RESEARCH

In the basement of the Stanford University Libraries, a robot the size of a sports utility vehicle is rapidly scanning books into digital form. The immediate plan is to transfer books published by Stanford University Press into digital form. Working with Google, the long-range goal is to turn the libraries' eight-million-volume collection into electronic form.

Scholarly books play an essential role in the research process for many subject areas regardless of whether they are ebooks or traditional print books. There is currently a concerted effort throughout the world to turn older books into digital form and to publish new books electronically in order to make them more widely available. Hundreds of thousands of books have been scanned or created in digital form, but they remain a small tip of the iceberg in terms of the total number of books. This is partly due to the sheer volume of books that have been published, and also because copyright issues have hindered some electronic publishing efforts. In some cases print might be a more suitable medium. Some scholars argue that ebooks make sense for reference books, computer science manuals, and science, legal, and business books, where information changes frequently and only small portions of the text are consulted. Lynch

(2001) and others argue that people still desire print when they need to read a book cover to cover.

In some fields, such as the sciences, information is being developed at such a rapid pace that the reliance on books to gather knowledge is diminishing in favor of journal articles and even preprint publications where articles are offered free on the internet prior to publication. The publication process for the printed book is simply too slow to benefit researchers working in fields where knowledge changes rapidly. Perhaps when the problems associated with ebooks are resolved, researchers in the sciences will again embrace the book. It is also possible that the transformation of a print book into an online format might evolve into another entity altogether. Some current ebook collections break books out into chapters or sections to provide better subject access to these collections, thus changing the definition of what constitutes a "book."

With that said, there is still a place for the book, regardless of format, in scholarly research, and even more so in undergraduate research. Because of their broad and deep nature, scholarly books provide a place where a topic can be fully explored, where knowledge can be pulled together and evaluated, and where detailed new research can be reported and analyzed. This chapter explains:

- why books can often provide a shortcut for researchers;
- what different types of books are available;
- how to find different types of books and ebooks;
- how to critically evaluate books.

USE BOOKS AS A SHORTCUT

Books provide a shortcut in the research process. This may seem counterintuitive. Why read a three-hundred-page scholarly tome when you can find a web page or a journal article that covers the same topic in a much shorter format? Books provide a broad and deep overview of a topic and the publishing process provides some assurances that the work is reputable. Journal articles often focus on one very specific aspect of a topic, and free web pages can sometimes be unreliable or biased.

If you are researching anorexia, a journal article might cover evidence of a limbic system imbalance in early-onset anorexia. If you have just started your research, this type of article will be too specific for your immediate needs. Finding out about the limbic system or early-onset anorexia may be appropriate in the later stages of your research, but you must first investigate the larger picture. What does recent research tell us about the causes and cures of anorexia? In what direction is future research headed?

What do top scholars who have spent decades studying anorexia have to say? A recent comprehensive book or subject encyclopedia will provide this information.

Finding a web page on anorexia might provide you with a more concise overview of the topic than getting a book, but finding a reputable *scholarly* web page can be challenging. Because the web, unlike libraries and publishers, has no filtering process, you must determine whether the site you have found is scholarly, authoritative, and unbiased. Published journal articles and books go through a rigorous editorial process and are often peer-reviewed, a process involving colleagues evaluating an author's work before it is published. The published source might appear on the web as an ebook or ejournal article, or in print, but it is distinguished from a web page by the fact that it is "published" in the traditional sense and has therefore undergone this vetting process. In addition, academic libraries carefully select the most scholarly and relevant books and journals for their collections, so a second filter not available on the free web is also in place when you limit your search to the items owned by an academic library.

By using a recently published scholarly book or subject encyclopedia, the researcher can get a snapshot of the current research on a particular topic, the major players that are investigating that topic, and the broader context within which the research topic falls.

USE A SUBJECT ENCYCLOPEDIA TO START YOUR RESEARCH

Subject encyclopedias provide a concise overview of the current state of research on a particular topic. Unlike a general encyclopedia such as *Encyclopedia Britannica*, subject encyclopedias focus on one topic. They can be broadly focused like the *McGraw-Hill Encyclopedia of Science and Technology*, or they can focus on specific subjects like the *Encyclopedia of Alcoholism*.

Subject encyclopedias are valuable for two reasons:

1. They provide a concise overview of research findings on a particular topic.
2. They provide a brief annotated list of the key books and articles on a subject area.

In the digital environment it is all too easy to find five thousand web sites or even two hundred books on a topic such as the Persian Gulf War. But to find the most important and influential works on this war, a subject encyclopedia is essential. Perhaps the ideal when starting a research paper is for your instructor to hand you a list of the most important books on that topic by the most reputable scholars in the field. Often that is not possible, so the subject encyclopedia provides a similar service. The subject encyclopedia provides a filter: in addition to giving you an overview of the research being conducted on a particular topic, it focuses on the most important books and articles. You can then avoid wading through the hundreds of resources that are available on your topic and focus on key works. Using filters is an essential component to the ongoing task of critical evaluation that needs to take place at every stage of the research process.

A subject encyclopedia can also assist you in narrowing your topic area. Browse the appropriate subject encyclopedia to see how much research exists on your subject. For example, if your topic is organized crime, use the *Encyclopedia of Organized Crime* to narrow your topic to a more manageable size. Do you want to write about the DeCavalcante family that inspired the HBO show *The Sopranos*? Or perhaps you would like to limit your research to a certain time period or geographic area by focusing on La Cosa Nostra in New York.

A subject encyclopedia is useful for beginning your research process, but you may not end up citing it in your final paper. Its purpose is to give an overview and bibliography so that you can get the lay of the land and focus on the key resources quickly. Check the publication date of your subject encyclopedia. A subject encyclopedia that is more than five years old might be useful for a research paper on Shakespeare, but less useful for a research paper on genetics where current knowledge changes rapidly.

Find a Subject Encyclopedia

There are several ways to find a subject encyclopedia. Most subject encyclopedias are still in print form, but more are becoming available online.

Use your library online catalog keyword search function. Try several synonyms or broader and narrower terms that cover your topic and combine them with the words "encyclopedia or handbook or dictionary or guide." For example:

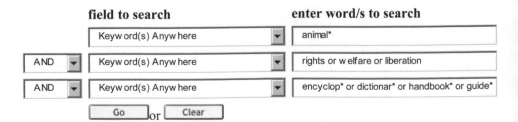

The "*" is used to retrieve both the plural and singular—title words would be singular but the subject heading for these terms uses the plural. The words "encyclopedia" and "dictionary" are often used interchangeably. Some dictionaries resemble encyclopedias because they have lengthy contextual entries, and some encyclopedias resemble dictionaries because they provide brief definitions.

Ask a reference librarian for a good subject encyclopedia on your topic. Many libraries now have live chat (IM) reference services and email reference, as well as help that is available in person. Check your library web site to connect with a reference librarian.

Consult a reference book of reference books. *The ARBA Guide to Subject Encyclopedias and Dictionaries* or *Subject Encyclopedias User Guide, Review Citations, and Keyword Index* provide extensive lists and information about available subject encyclopedias. Remember to broaden or narrow your topic area if you have trouble finding a subject encyclopedia specifically on your topic.

USE BIBLIOGRAPHIES AND WEB GUIDES TO LOCATE KEY RESOURCES

Bibliographies are lists of books, articles, web sites, and other resources that have been gathered together and summarized in a book, web site, or journal article. Book bibliographies often provide extensive lists of relevant resources on a particular topic. A summary is provided for each resource listed. Bibliographies are useful for doing comprehensive research on a topic or for scanning to find out which titles might be most appropriate for you to follow up on for your research. Scholarly bibliographies can help the researcher avoid getting buried in resources. Instead of the scholar having to search the online catalog or the web by subject, using a bibliography identifies a selection of the important resources and a description of the contents of each book or article listed.

More scholars and librarians are providing bibliographies or "subject guides"—selective lists of resources about a topic—on the web. They often do not provide annotations and they must be carefully evaluated, but frequently they can be useful. Unlike a book bibliography that has gone through a rigorous publishing process to ensure reliability, web bibliographies are self-published. At a minimum, check to see that the author of the site has some expertise or credentials in the area covered, and that the site or the author is connected to a reputable institution or scholarly organization.

Find Bibliographies and Web Subject Guides

To find a published bibliography on your topic, search the library online catalog. Use the keyword search feature and type in your topic and the word "bibliography." If possible, limit the search for the word "bibliography" to the subject heading area of each record in the catalog by selecting "subject" instead of "keyword" in the search boxes. Online library catalogs work differently, but most provide a pull-down box that allows you to select the field in the catalog you want to search, such as keyword (anywhere), title, author, and subject (assigned Library of Congress Subject Heading). To find a bibliography of critical works on Yeats, search:

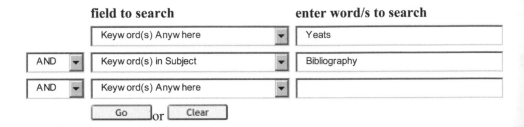

To find a web subject guide created by a librarian or scholar, use a major search engine such as Google and type in your topic followed by the word "bibliography." Using the word "bibliography" cuts out many of the meta-sites (lists of links on a topic) created by students and laypeople, and increases your chances of finding a scholarly site written by a professor or librarian with subject expertise in your area. In a Google advanced search, you can limit your domain to an educational institution by typing "EDU" in the domain box. Be specific when you type in your subject:

> sea turtles and bibliography

If you retrieve nothing useful, broaden your topic:

> marine biology and bibliography

USE REFERENCE BOOKS TO LOCATE QUICK FACTUAL INFORMATION

Reference books are used to look up information, facts, and data or to get a brief overview or definition of a topic. More reference works are migrating to electronic form, a perfect format because most researchers only need to skim a few pages at one sitting. (Biographical reference sources are covered in chapter 5 and statistical reference sources are covered in chapter 7.)

- **General Encyclopedias,** such as the *Encyclopedia Britannica Online*, provide information about a topic, event, or person. They are perfect for checking a date, historical event, or other factual information quickly. They are used to gain a contextual understanding of a topic or to verify a fact, but are not usually cited directly in research papers, usually because a fact (e.g., the starting date of World War II) is so well established it does not need to be cited.

- **Subject Dictionaries** provide definitions and explanations of key concepts and terms used in a particular field of study. For example, *The Oxford Dictionary of Economics* provides one-paragraph definitions of terms in that field such as "dollar standard" and "external labor market" that a general dictionary would not include. Unlike encyclopedias, dictionaries do not provide contextual information, but only provide a brief definition of a term.

- **Directories** have contact information and descriptions of organizations, associations, or companies. Although contact information can often be found on the web, directories provide unique advantages: *The Directory of Consultants in Environmental Science* brings together all the consultants that work in the field of environmental science; and *Peterson's Four-Year Colleges*, which provides separate indexes for majors offered, geographic locations, and names of institutions.

- **Atlases and Gazetteers** provide geographical and spatial information of many different types. Atlases are often more than just maps—they can provide historical information or offer themes such as the *Atlas of the Crusades*. Gazetteers are dictionaries listing geographical names and places with definitions and information about them.

- **Handbooks and Manuals** contain surveys of a particular subject area or discipline. These types of works provide factual and statistical information. Some handbooks, especially in the sciences, provide data compilations. Examples of these are the *CRC Handbook of Chemistry and Physics* and the *Merck Index*. Important multi-volume handbooks often provide critically evaluated data—data that has either been compared with that reported in the literature or developed empirically.

- **Almanacs and Yearbooks** provide a compendium of information on current or historical people, places, events, and subjects. *The New York Public Library Desk Reference* and the *Information Please* almanacs provide brief information on an enormous array of subjects such as famous historical speeches, weights and measures, and crime statistics.

- **Chronologies** consist of a historical timeline that can provide the researcher with the context in which an event took place. The *Chronology and Fact Book of the United Nations* and the *Chronology of African-American History*, for example, provide researchers in those areas with a timeline of important events.

FIND REFERENCE BOOKS

Most reference books are still in print form, though more are becoming available in ebook form. The following describes how to find print, library-owned ebook, and free ebook reference books.

Find Print Reference Books

There are three ways to find print reference books.

1. Keyword search the online catalog. For example, if you are looking for a dictionary that defines terminology used in psychology, try searching:

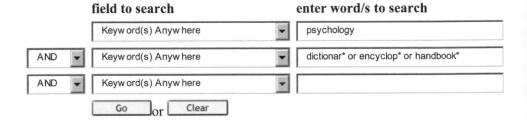

The "*" is used to retrieve both the plural and singular—title words would be singular, but the subject heading for these terms uses the plural. The terms "dictionary," "encyclopedia," and "handbook" are often used interchangeably, so it is important to include all of them. Some encyclopedias, such as the *Encyclopedia of Gods*, resemble dictionaries and provide short definitions of terms. Other dictionaries, such as the *Palgrave Dictionary of Economics*, resemble encyclopedias and provide longer entries and contextual information about broader concepts and trends. Other keywords used for particular types of reference books include "chronology," "almanac," "atlas," and so on.

2. Use the *Guide to Reference Books* edited by Robert Balay (1996). This bible of reference books provides a comprehensive guide and index to available reference books published before 1996. Because many of the books it covers have subsequent editions, it remains a useful source. It is found at the reference desk at most libraries.

3. Ask a reference librarian for assistance. Reference librarians are experts at finding both print and electronic reference sources in all fields.

Find Library-Owned Electronic Reference Books

Most libraries provide a separate web page with links to the online reference ebooks that they own as well as other reference sources available free via the web. Most academic library web sites include a link to a web page called "Reference Tools" or "Electronic Reference Works," or they include their electronic reference book collections in their list of databases or electronic resources. Individual titles are usually cataloged in library on-line catalogs as well. Consult a reference librarian if you have trouble locating the electronic reference collection. Electronic resources of any kind that are owned by a library are usually only available via that library's web page to someone who is affiliated with the institution.

Find Free Electronic Reference Books

Some of the larger collections of electronic reference books and other reference tools on the web are so enormous or advertisement-saturated that they can be less than useful. Some academic and public libraries have set up meta-sites of collected links to free, reputable electronic reference tools. These sites are easier to navigate to find quality resources. The following are some of the most useful meta-sites listing these free tools.

Brown University
http://www.brown.edu/Facilities/University_Library/vrc

Chicago Public Library
http://cpl.lib.uic.edu/008subject/005genref/readyref.html

Internet Public Library
http://www.ipl.org

University of Texas
http://www.lib.utexas.edu/refsites/index.html

USE SCHOLARLY BOOKS FOR A BROAD AND DEEP OVERVIEW

Experts, frequently university professors, write scholarly books called monographs to further the state of knowledge about a subject. These works usually contain extensive bibliographies—lists of resources cited in the book—that connect a scholar's work to earlier research by other scholars. These books are published by scholarly presses, often university presses such as Harvard University Press or Oxford University Press. They can be challenging to read because they use language specific to a particular discipline such as economics or biology. Scholarly books are sometimes available in ebook form, but many are only available in print.

Scholars frequently write books to pull together and analyze previous research in a wider context and format than is available within the confines of a twenty-page journal article. A journal article on genetics would likely focus on a specific area of research such as population genetics of threatened wild plants in Japan, whereas a scholarly book provides researchers with the big picture in terms of current trends in genetics research.

Most scholarly books are carefully selected, screened, edited, and evaluated by editors with assistance from other scholars. This ensures that the research presented in a book is noteworthy, accurate, carefully analyzed, and written in a clear manner. Unlike most web sites, the publishing process a book undergoes adds to the likelihood that the book accurately reflects not only the scholar's research, but previous research that forms the base on which this new research is added.

Scholarly books are often an essential part of the research process. A two-page paper on drug use in suburban high schools can usually be handled by gathering a few journal articles together on that topic; but for any substantial research paper it would be essential to cite recent books (except in certain science disciplines where books are outdated by the time they are published).

Supplement Scholarly Books with Popular and Trade Books

Popular and trade books often report on information that originates in more scholarly works. They are written in a less formal or technical way and are easier to read than scholarly books. In a way they are "translations" of more scholarly research into language that can be deciphered by an educated layperson.

Popular and trade books provide varying amounts of documentation on the information they report. Some have lengthy bibliographies of scholarly sources and are probably more reliable, while others have an informal tone and do not cite any research and should be used with caution. Large publishers such as Random House, as well as smaller publishers such as Dharma Publishing, produce trade books. The reliability of these books does not necessarily correlate with the size of the publishing house, though some smaller presses have particular political or religious agendas that might produce less objective books.

Popular books can be useful and even essential when conducting research on current trends or popular culture, but they should be evaluated carefully and validated by other more scholarly sources.

Find Scholarly and Popular Books

Scholarly books as well as other types of books can be located using the following steps.

Use Your Library Online Catalog

What do *Socrates*, *Einstein*, and *Josiah* all have in common? All are on-line library catalogs listing the resources owned by a particular library.[1] Most academic libraries have an enormous database that contains a record for each of the resources—books, journals, videos, and special collections—that the library owns. These catalogs are frequently given a name that relates in some way to the institution with which the library is affiliated, though sometimes they are just referred to as the "library catalog." A library's catalog can usually be found prominently displayed on the library home page on the web.

Search the Catalog

If you already know the title or author of a book you are looking for, type it into the search box and limit your search to the field you would like to search, such as "author" or "title." In order to search the catalog by subject or keyword, it is important to use synonyms and Boolean searching—combining similar terms with the word "or" and combining different criteria for your search with the word "and." For example, if you are looking for books about women athletes you would search:

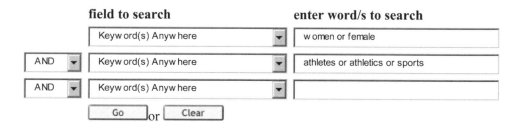

Broaden or Narrow Your Search

Broaden your search if you find very few results. In the above example this would mean adding more synonyms or dropping one of your search criteria and just searching for books about sports, hoping that some of these books would include information about women athletes. If your search retrieves too many items, narrow the search by using fewer synonyms or by adding other criteria. In this case you might replace the words "athletes," "athletics," and "sports" with "soccer" if you only wanted to retrieve books on women and soccer. Or, you could limit your search to a time period or country to narrow the search results.

Browse the Stacks and the Catalog

In the movie *High Fidelity*, John Cusack's character arranges his music collection chronologically by the woman he was dating when he bought the music. This allowed him to locate music easily by associating it with a particular girlfriend and time period. Fortunately, libraries use a more broadly accepted though still imperfect system of classification by subject area. Most academic libraries use the Library of Congress (LC) classification system, while many public and school libraries use the Dewey Decimal system. Both systems bring "like" items together with some success. The LC system[2] breaks all knowledge into twenty broad categories indicated by a letter of the alphabet—for example, literature is "P." Each category is then broken down further so that American literature is "PS." You do not need to understand the LC system to use the library, you just need to know the following:

- Like objects are found together. If you look up a book on gun control in the online catalog and then go to the stacks to find it by call number, other books about that same topic will be sitting next to it.
- Because many books can be classified under several different subject areas, not *all* books on a topic will be sitting next to each other. A book on women's legal rights could be in a law section or a women's studies section.
- When you find a book on your topic in the online catalog, the record for the book will list the three or four LC Subject Headings assigned to that book. Pick the most useful ones and browse the catalog by clicking on an LC Subject Heading or typing the heading into the catalog and searching by subject.

LC is a complex and useful system. Take advantage of it by browsing the books on either side of any book you are retrieving from the library shelves. Also remember to use synonyms and think of other keywords to use in the online catalog to discover all the books on your topic. Many veteran researchers have experienced the serendipity that can occur when browsing the stacks. While retrieving a book on a particular topic the eye falls on a related topic and suddenly new creative connections about a research problem can occur. Browsing the shelves as well as learning to browse the catalog are important early stages of the research process. Faculty rely on browsing more than undergraduates because they already have knowledge in the field that they can apply to their browsing (such as familiarity with important publishers and key author names in their field).

Use Other Library Catalogs

If your library does not have a strong collection in the area that you are researching, connect to LibWeb (sunsite.berkeley.edu/Libweb) and choose a library catalog that might have a better collection of books in your area. If you are searching for books and articles about Catholicism, Georgetown University and Boston College—both of which were founded as Jesuit institutions—are apt to have stronger collections in this area. Use the interlibrary loan form, usually found on your library web page, to request that your library borrow any books that you need that are not owned by your library.

Use *WorldCat* or *RedLightGreen*

WorldCat and *RedLightGreen* are separate databases that merge the holdings of hundreds of library catalogs. *RedLightGreen* is available for free on the web (http://www.RedLightGreen.com) and merges the catalogs of more than 150 libraries and other memory institutions in the Research Libraries Group. *WorldCat* is available on the "Databases" or "Electronic Resources" page through subscription at many academic libraries. *WorldCat* provides access to hundreds of library catalogs from the United States and several other countries. If you are looking for a comprehensive list of *almost* all books published on a particular topic, *WorldCat* and *RedLightGreen* come closer than any other source. Both function similarly to your own library online catalog, and both provide information about which libraries own a particular title.

USE EBOOKS FOR RESEARCH

Ebooks are regularly purchased by academic libraries and can be found by searching the library online catalog or by consulting the "databases" or "online resources" web page at your library. The most common ebooks are science, medical, law, business, and computer literature, as well as reference works. These books lend themselves more naturally to ebook form because of their need for frequent updates and because they are often consulted in part rather than read cover to cover. Some of the larger academic collections include *Netlibrary, Ebrary, ScienceDirect, Oxford Reference Online, Gale Virtual Reference Library, Safari*, and *Ebooks Library (EBL)*.

In addition to ebooks that are purchased by libraries or the public, there are many ebooks that are available for free over the web, typically because they are older and their copyright has expired or because they are published by the U.S. government and not subject to copyright.

Two large gateway sites provide access to many of the free ebooks available on the web. Also, University of Texas Libraries has compiled a list of ebook collections arranged by discipline (http://www.lib.utexas.edu/books/etext.html).

Online Books Page
http://onlinebooks.library.upenn.edu
Hosted at the University of Pennsylvania Library, the Online Books Page provides an index to books and collections that are freely available on the web.

The Digital Book Index
http://www.digitalbookindex.com
This site provides links to over 100,000 books from more than 1,800 commercial and noncommercial collections. More than half the books are available for free, many others are available for a modest fee.

DO NOT READ THE ENTIRE BOOK

Studies have shown that even professors often do not read entire books that they use for their research (Summerfield, Mandel, and Kantor 1999). When you find a book on your topic, develop an efficient system for determining how much, if any, of the book you need to read.

- Scan the table of contents and index
- Look up aspects of your topic in the index to see if they are covered
- Skim the preface, introduction, and conclusion
- Read over the bibliography: what resources is this book citing?
- Determine which chapters might be the most useful to read in their entirety by scanning chapter subheadings

For subject encyclopedias and other types of reference books read only the section that is relevant to your topic.

DON'T USE BOOKS IF . . .

If you are doing research in a cutting-edge area of science or are investigating a recent phenomenon, you may not want to consult any books. Many faculty and graduate students in the hard sciences, such as molecular biology or genetics, rarely consult books due to the swiftly changing nature of scientific investigations. A book can take as long as a year after the author finished writing it to become available to the public.

In the sciences, journal literature is the primary means of communication and debate of new ideas. Books may be used, but only peripherally, as a means of locating references to journal articles detailing the original research. A biochemist working on the structure of a particular protein would not consult a book because more current and detailed information would be found in the journal articles written by other researchers in that field. Similarly, current political events or cultural activities that are taking place have not yet been analyzed and written about in book form. However, for research of most political events and social trends, consulting books remains important. Putting the current political uprising or medical epidemic into context, researching how past events have been evaluated, and building on conclusions drawn by previous scholars about similar events is crucial to the research process.

USE FILTERING DEVICES TO DEAL WITH INFORMATION OVERLOAD

Finding too many titles on a topic is more common than finding too few. Using filtering devices will help you narrow your search in a logical rather than haphazard way and will result in higher quality resources. You may not be aware of it, but by searching an academic library catalog, you are using a filter. The library carefully selects which books are worthy of inclusion in an academic library depending on the research needs of its community. The library does not usually buy the latest Stephen King novel, unless it has a strong popular culture department on campus. Following is a list of useful filtering techniques.

- Use a bibliography or subject encyclopedia. These tools, mentioned earlier in this chapter, provide selective lists of books deemed important on a specific topic.
- Ask your professor or instructor, or any other expert with whom you might have a connection for recommendations. Rather than wading through the two hundred books your online catalog turns up, ask an expert what he or she might suggest. Studies have shown that most faculty locate books and articles by conferring with a colleague when investigating an area outside of their own immediate area of expertise (Summerfield, Mandel, and Kantor 1999).
- Use the list of references at the back of a book or article that you have already found on your topic. If you do this each time you discover a book or article on your topic, once you have found dozens of articles on a specific topic you will begin to see the same titles and authors mentioned repeatedly. This is one way to find the key works about your research area. What is most important is usually what is being cited the most in the literature on that topic.

CRITICALLY EVALUATE BOOKS

Evaluating books and deciding whether to use them in your research is crucial. Which books you select will affect the quality of your own research and the conclusions you reach. Not citing a prominent authority who writes frequently in the area you are studying will appear as a glaring hole in your research to a faculty member familiar with the subject.

Critical evaluation involves two steps. The first is the mechanical process articulated below. It involves a checklist that includes the reputation of the author, the publisher, and the language of the text, as well as book reviews that indicate how a work was received. The second step is the development over time of a "knowledge bank" of your own about a research topic and discipline. After studying, for example, the effects of certain pesticides on ground water, and after reading a few dozen books and articles on this topic, your knowledge bank begins to develop.

Most advanced graduate students and faculty have already developed this knowledge bank and rely on it heavily and almost subconsciously for all of their work. The knowledge bank includes a working understanding of the topic itself, a familiarity with the reputation of scholarly journals that frequently publish on this topic, and an understanding of the most commonly published experts in this area. It also includes the ability to recognize a quality research design in the field, and the degree to which the research builds on previous findings and cites authoritative researchers in that subject area. Most importantly, the work advanced researchers have done themselves—reading and evaluating claims that their colleagues have put forward—has added to the depth of their knowledge about a topic.

Consider the following questions when reviewing any book and add your own knowledge about a topic into the mix.

Examine the Author

What are the author's credentials? Is the author a journalist writing a trade book, or is the author an expert (scholar, university professor) in the particular area he or she is covering? Has your instructor mentioned this author? Have you seen the author's name cited in other articles or books on this topic? Is the author associated with a particular organization or institution? What are the goals of this organization or institution? Look in the front or back of the book to see if it includes a brief paragraph about the author. If not, try a web search to find out a little more about the author or look at chapter 5 on biographical information for help locating information about an author.

Note the Currency

Is the date current enough for your topic? Information about research areas in rapidly changing fields, especially in the sciences, often need to be very current, whereas it can sometimes be beneficial to have a somewhat older, more established source when working in the humanities. Is the book a second or third edition? Numerous editions can indicate that the work has become a standard source and might be more reliable.

Evaluate the Publisher

If a university press or scholarly society (e.g., American Historical Association) published the book, that indicates that the resource is of a scholarly, rather than popular, nature. If a more mainstream or popular publisher released the book, use more caution in choosing to include it in your research project.

Determine the Content

Skim the preface and table of contents. Who is the intended audience? What is the purpose of the publication? Is the language aimed at high school students, or does it contain more discipline-specific language? Is the information being presented as fact or opinion? Are statements supported by evidence? Does there seem to be a bias or slant to the writing? Does the language sound emotional or objective?

Check the Bibliography

Does the book have a bibliography? Does the bibliography cite known authorities in the field? Is it an extensive bibliography or does it contain just a few references? Are the citations to scholarly or popular resources? For example, are there a few citations to *Newsweek* magazine, or are there many citations to articles in journals such as the *Journal of American History*?

Compare and Corroborate

Compare the book you find with other books or articles you have read on this topic. Do the findings in this book agree with other research that has been conducted?

Use Reviews to Evaluate a Book

The best way to critically evaluate a book is often to let experts in the field do the work for you. Not all scholarly books are reviewed, but many, especially the more important ones, are reviewed. The fact that a scholarly book has been reviewed should be one more piece of evidence that it is a worthwhile work to consider in your research. Book reviews provide a feel for the critical reception of a particular title as well as a better sense of the background of the author. At a minimum most reviews provide a summary of the book, and many reviews provide evaluative information and lay out the historical or theoretical context of the arguments made in the book. It is usually wise to look up at least two reviews if possible, because occasionally one review will be particularly slanted and not provide an objective and accurate reflection of the contents of the book.

Find Online and Print Book Reviews

The resources listed below are owned by most academic libraries and can be keyword searched by the author and title of the book. In some databases a box can be checked on the search screen to indicate that you are looking for a review, but usually this is not necessary unless the author name and title are extremely common words. Remember that you are looking for a book review (i.e., an article), not the book itself. Books are usually reviewed the year they are published or the following year. Because the dates of coverage vary for each database, choose a database that covers the appropriate date range for your book.

To find a resource go to your library web page and look for a page called "Databases" or "Articles" or "E-resources" within your library web site. If your library does not own the electronic version of the article, it will frequently have the same article in print. Use the library online catalog to find the print version of a title if there is not a direct link to the full text from the database.

Academic Search Premier/Academic Search Elite/Ebsco

This large online collection contains articles from thousands of magazines, journals, and newspapers. It includes a large number of book reviews from 1990 to the present. Many of the articles are available in full text online. For some titles only citations are available and the journal must be looked up in the online catalog.

Book Review Digest

This resource provides summaries of reviews from about ninety popular magazines for American and British books published from 1983 to the present. Earlier book reviews can be found in the print version of this title. It is not the best source for scholarly reviews. Many libraries have the online version of this title.

Book Review Index

This title provides citations to reviews from five hundred journals and newspapers. Some of the journals are scholarly, such as the *Harvard Busi-*

ness Review, and some are popular, such as *Time*. The reviews date back to 1969. The title is available in print or online at most libraries.

Infotrac/Expanded Academic

Infotrac has several different versions and is called by different titles. It provides citations and in many cases full-text articles including book reviews for thousands of journals, magazines, and newspapers.

JSTOR

JSTOR contains the full text of hundreds of important scholarly journals in many disciplines. Many of these journals include book review sections. The most recent years of each journal are not available in this database, but many titles go back several decades or more, so it is useful for retrieving reviews of older books.

LexisNexis

This resource provides full-text articles from hundreds of newspapers, journals, and magazines. Dates of coverage vary for each title included. It is especially strong for newspaper, business, and legal resources.

Proquest

This resource provides citations and full-text articles for thousands of journals, magazines, and newspapers, many of which contain book reviews.

Readers' Guide to Periodical Literature

This title provides citations to reviews and other articles from about two hundred popular magazines.

Web of Science

This large, comprehensive citation index provides citations to scholarly book reviews, as well as citations to other journal articles in all disciplines.

Try to find more than one review about a book to get a more even critique. Sometimes a book may be panned in one publication and applauded in another. Bring your own judgment into play when you read a review. How does the review jell with your reaction to the book?

Books provide the researcher with a breadth and depth not available in journal articles. By carefully selecting which books to use for your research, the quality of your final product is greatly improved.

NOTES

1. *Socrates* is the name of the library catalog at Stanford University, *Einstein* is at Rochester Institute of Technology, and *Josiah* is at Brown University.

2. The complete Library of Congress classification can be found at http://www.loc.gov/catdir/cpso/lcco/lcco.html.

REFERENCES

Balay, Robert ed., 1996. *Guide to reference books*. Chicago: American Library Association.

Lynch, Clifford. 2001. The battle to define the future of the book in the digital world. *First Monday* 6, no. 6 (June). http://firstmonday.org/issues/issue6_6/lynch/index.html. Accessed December 1, 2004.

Summerfield, Mary, Carol Mandel, and Paul Kantor. 1999. *Final report of the online books evaluation project*, Columbia University (December). http://www.columbia.edu/cu/libraries/digital/texts/about.html. Accessed December 4, 2003.

3

Scholarly and Popular Articles

Ideas should freely spread from one to another over the globe.

Thomas Jefferson

Research findings are published in scholarly journals. Magazines, newspapers, and other more informal sources on the web also report on research findings and provide other news and information. The challenge for the researcher is to survive the tidal wave of articles and unearth the most relevant, reliable, and objective titles. This often means choosing more scholarly articles and fewer popular and informal sources.

More than ten thousand different scholarly journals are published every year, and the number continues to rise. This proliferation is due in part to the "publish or perish" system in academia, where professors are judged and granted tenure partly based on their publishing output. Competition and a deepening awareness of the complexity of knowledge have also driven researchers to pursue increasingly specialized areas of study, thereby generating more and more focused journals such as:

- *The Journal of Articles in Support of the Null Hypothesis*
- *The Journal of Circadian Rhythms*
- *The George Eliot Review*

In addition to journals, an even greater number of magazines and newspapers are generated annually. These range from low-end tabloids that rely on questionable journalism to high quality newspapers that are carefully fact-checked, such as the *New York Times*. The number of magazines continues to increase as more specialized interests and market niches are un-covered. Add to this the more than three million estimated blogs[1] and the full picture emerges of an unfathomable number of resources to navigate (Weber 2004).

This tremendous number of articles combined with the ease of access to information via the web has led to a glut of information where quality research easily gets buried and free or easy-to-locate resources compete for attention with more valuable studies. This is not to say that free resources necessarily have less value than subscription resources. There are a number of high quality research journals available for free over the web through the Open Access movement.[2] But many more journals are only accessible through library or personal subscriptions. With a little knowledge and experience, the best articles can be retrieved using the resources available from your library web page.

This chapter will explain how to:

- identify scholarly journal articles and decide when to use journal articles and when to use magazine and newspaper articles;
- select appropriate article databases to search for articles;
- develop effective search strategies when searching these databases;
- locate the full text of articles;
- evaluate articles;
- understand the role of informal information sources in the research process.

IDENTIFY AND USE SCHOLARLY JOURNAL ARTICLES

The purpose, author expertise, writing style, appearance, length, and vo-cabulary differ greatly between scholarly journals and other periodicals such as magazines and newspapers. Scholars cite journal articles and books in their own research to demonstrate the connection between their research and the prior research of others. This ties their work into the scholarly con-versation that is taking place about a particular topic and also provides an authoritative source for a claim, statistic, definition, or discovery. Scholars also cite magazine and newspaper articles, though less frequently. Some-times these popular articles are cited when a topic being investigated is ex-tremely recent or when the research relates to a local news event.

Scholarly journal articles are the essential resource for reporting the find-ings of academic research. Professors or other experts specializing in a par-ticular discipline or area of study write journal articles. For any substantive research paper, it is essential to include information from at least some journal articles.

Journal articles provide more recent research findings than books because books take longer to write and publish. Journal articles also provide a more focused analysis of a specific topic. It would be unusual to find a journal article on daycare, for example, as this topic is too broad and would more likely be covered in a book. A journal article on daycare might focus on a specific aspect of daycare, such as the impact of time spent in daycare on the language development of toddlers.

In addition, scholarly articles typically contain extensive bibliographies (lists of citations) on which the research is based. The articles are written for a limited audience of other scholars and students in the field. Journals have minimal advertising and pictures, other than graphs and tables. They tend to be more plain-looking than magazines, whether online or in print. The writing style can be more technical and complex than that found in popular magazines. Journals are frequently written in a formal style that reflects the language and methodology of the discipline. For example, an article in an experimental psychology journal would follow the typical pattern that is common in that field:

- title
- abstract
- background
- research methodology/procedure
- results and discussion
- references

USE MAGAZINE AND NEWSPAPER ARTICLES WHEN APPROPRIATE

Journalists, staff, and freelance writers generate the bulk of magazine and newspaper articles. Many journalists are generalists—they may specialize in a particular area of the news such as health or politics, but they do not have the academic credentials or research background related to a field of study or academic discipline. The writing style of magazines and newspapers is informal, non-technical, accessible, and concise.

Magazine and newspaper articles often report on current topics, including summaries of the results of recent research. Many magazines have a focus such as music or politics, while many newspapers specialize in current news or entertainment occurring in specific geographic locations. Articles in magazines and newspapers reflect contemporary opinions and reactions to events as they are unfolding. They can be useful for current as well as historical research when augmented by more scholarly sources. Writers for magazines and newspapers are less likely to base their articles on research and rarely provide citations or contain bibliographies listing research articles or books.

Differences between:	
Journal Articles	**Magazine Articles**
Scholarly	Popular
Written by professors, experts	Written by journalists
Lengthy: 10–30 pages	Brief: 1–5 pages
Extensive bibliography	Usually no bibliography
Plain, few graphics	Colorful, lots of graphics
Little advertising	Advertising
Technical, specialized language	Nontechnical, accessible language
Audience: scholars	Audience: laypeople
Report research findings	Entertain and provide information

CHOOSE DATABASES TO SEARCH FOR ARTICLES

General and specialized databases—not online library catalogs—provide access to the content found within articles. Some databases provide the full-text article immediately, while others link to the full text. A third category provides just a citation and abstract (summary) of the article. In this last case the user needs to use the library online catalog to see if the title is available or needs to be borrowed from another institution using an inter-library loan form.

There are three types of article databases.

1. **Large multidisciplinary aggregators** provide access to an enormous and di-verse range of journal, magazine, and newspaper articles. The full text of the articles is frequently available in the database.
2. **Federated search engines,** not yet available on all library web sites, merge and search the contents of many different types of databases, including multidis-ciplinary aggregators (#1 above) and specialized article databases (#3 below).
3. **Specialized article databases** provide citations and in some cases the full text of articles in journals from a specific discipline or subject area such as psy-chology or anthropology.

Use Large Multidisciplinary Aggregators to Find Articles

Aggregators pull articles together from a wide variety of sources. They provide the advantage of "one-stop shopping" by letting the researcher search one engine for any topic. They are often a useful place to begin research, and for shorter research papers and multidisciplinary research they may be the only tool needed. They provide access to journals as well as magazines and newspapers.

The disadvantages of large aggregators are that they may include access to thousands of journals, magazines, and newspapers, but they may not be the most comprehensive tool for a specific topic. For example, a large article database of three thousand journals and magazines might include thirty sociology journals, but a specialized article database such as *Sociological Abstracts* provides access to hundreds of journals in sociology and would be more appropriate for someone doing research in sociology. Aggregators can also flood the researcher with irrelevant titles because of their size and sometimes because of their lack of subject indexing. They also lack the powerful and precise search capabilities of more specialized subject databases.

Large Multidisciplinary Aggregator Databases

The following is a list of large article databases. All but two are subscription only. Many of these titles can be located by searching your library home page under "online resources" or "databases." Free resources are indicated with a URL.

Academic Search Premiere/Academic Search Elite/Ebsco—extensive collection of journals, magazines, and newspapers.
ArticlesFirst—indexes the table of contents of thousands of journals, magazines, and newspapers.
Directory of Open Access Journals—free index to large collection of free, open access journals. www.doaj.org.
Electronic Collections Online—extensive collection of scholarly journals.
Google Scholar[3]—a free index to a growing collection of scholarly materials, including articles; especially strong in certain scientific fields. http://scholar.google.com.
Infotrac/Expanded Academic—extensive collection of journals, magazines, and newspapers.
Ingenta—large collection of scholarly journals.
JSTOR—large collection of scholarly journals going back many decades; does not include issues from the most recent two years.
LexisNexis—extensive collection of newspapers, business and news magazines, legal journals, and law reviews.
Omnifile—large collection of journals and magazines.
Periodical Abstracts—large collection of journals and magazines.
Web of Science—extremely large index to journal literature with many valuable features, including the ability to track a journal article and find out if other journal articles cited the article after it was published.

Use Federated Search Engines to Find Articles

Federated search engines pull together and search the contents of many library subscription article databases as well as other resources. Not all libraries have a federated search engine, but more are being developed. These search engines have the advantage of being larger while also allowing the user to customize the search to focus on a particular discipline or broad subject area. The search engines lack many of the specialized search abilities and limiting devices of specific databases.

If your library has a federated search engine it will usually appear at the front of the list of databases or electronic/online resources, or it will be highlighted on the library home page. Libraries usually name the federated search engines using some variant of the word "meta" (e.g., metasearch) or "one" (e.g., "onesearch"), or another word indicating the concept of combined searching.

Use Specialized Article Databases to Find Articles

Several hundred article databases have been developed to locate specific types of journal articles. These specialized tools provide the researcher with a wonderful filter to focus on the most relevant and scholarly articles. Most tend to be more comprehensive for a particular discipline and cover almost all the scholarly journal articles written in that discipline. Some of these databases cover many decades and even a century of literature in a discipline, while others have earlier print counterparts that provide access to older materials. For most subjects it is better to use a specialized database than an aggregator or federated search engine. Many of these article databases pull together research in one discipline so that almost all anthropology articles can be found in *Anthropology Plus* and almost all American history journal articles can be found in *America: History and Life.*

Use the appendix to choose the specialized database that will be most appropriate for your needs. For comprehensive research you will want to search the two or three databases listed for the discipline in which you are working. For libraries that have developed federated (combined) search engines, the appropriate databases for each subject area will already be grouped together and can be searched at the same time by selecting the appropriate subject area from the federated search screen.

DEVELOP EFFECTIVE SEARCH STRATEGIES

Most article databases are becoming similar to Google. You can type in any word and the database is large enough so that you usually get some results. But to effectively search article databases it helps to learn a few search techniques. These techniques are not complicated. Skimming the paragraphs below and putting these steps to work can save an enormous amount of time by retrieving more relevant articles quickly. These techniques include:

1. using synonyms connected by the "or" operator to expand your search, and combining concepts with the "and" operator to narrow your search (Boolean searching);
2. using a truncation symbol (*) to catch different word endings;
3. using limits to narrow search results.

Use Boolean Searching

Article databases are not "smart." If you ask for "teenagers," a database will find articles containing that word, but if most articles on this topic use the word "adolescents," these relevant articles will not be retrieved. The example below illustrates how to use Boolean searching to retrieve all the relevant articles on a topic.

Research question: *Does watching movies cause teenagers to act violently?*

1. **Break your search into major concepts**

   Concepts: *Movies, Teenagers, Violence*

2. **Develop synonyms for each concept**

   Movies: films, motion pictures
   Teenagers: adolescents, youth
   Violence: aggression, hostility, fighting

3. **Combine synonyms with "or" and different concepts with "and"** (Boolean searching). These words can be put in search boxes provided by most article databases.

   "OR" retrieves one or more of the synonyms. Search results will have either the word "films," "movies," or "motion pictures," but not necessarily all of those words.
   "AND" will retrieve all concepts linked by "and." For example, "Films and Teenagers" will retrieve only records that have both terms present.

field to search   enter word/s to search

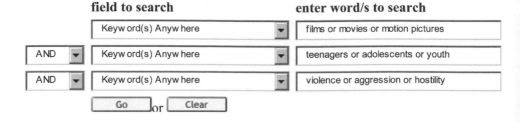

Too few results? Add synonyms for each concept.

Too many results? Drop some synonyms or add an additional concept. Synonyms can be entered into the same search box, while separate concepts need to be connected by "and," as in the example above. If only one search box is available, use "nesting," a process in which parentheses are used to dictate which searches should be performed first (i.e., synonyms—"or" searches—are done first, then concepts are combined):

(films or movies or motion pictures) and (teenagers or adolescents or youth) and (violence or aggression or hostility or fighting)

Use Truncation to Catch Word Endings or Alternative Spellings

Truncation symbols save time by retrieving alternative word endings. Most journal databases now use "*" to retrieve plurals and other word endings.

Type: dog* to retrieve dog or dogs
Type: adolescen* to retrieve adolescent or adolescence or adolescents

Limit Your Search to Retrieve More Relevant Results

Article databases have pull-down boxes that allow the searcher to limit the search in many ways. Federated search databases allow the user to limit by discipline and publication type (for example, you can search for biology journal articles only). Other limits, such as year published, language, and publication type, are frequently found in pull-down boxes described below.

Limit Search to Subject Heading or Descriptor

Humans index many specialized article databases by assigning several subject headings to describe each article. By limiting your search to look in just the subject heading or descriptor field of a record, you can greatly reduce the number of irrelevant search results—results that happen to have your keywords though the article was not actually about that topic. For example, a search for "insomnia" might retrieve articles that mention the word but are not really *about* insomnia generally. By limiting the search for "insomnia" to the subject heading only, articles that are focused on this topic will be retrieved.

In order to use subject headings or descriptors, you need to know what terms to use for the concept you are seeking. In the insomnia search, is the proper search term "insomnia" or "sleep disorders" or some other term? Different databases use different subject headings. One way to uncover the proper subject heading is to:

1. Do a keyword search using synonyms.
2. Skim the beginning of the list of articles until you find one good article.
3. Look at the full record for that article and note the subject headings used.
4. Return to the search screen, limit the search to "subject heading" by using the pull-down box, and enter the appropriate term.

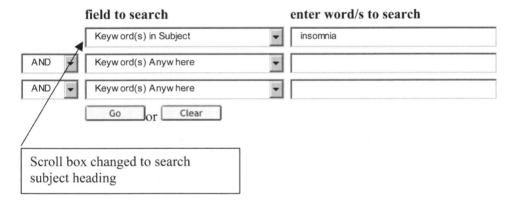

Subject terms are carefully developed to reflect the language and specificity of the discipline covered in a particular database. Just as Inuits have many words to describe snow, a women's studies database will have several different ways of indexing the term "discrimination" in order to catch different uses, while an education database will use many different, nuanced terms for "learning."

Limit Your Search to Phrases

Many databases use quotation marks around phrases to limit the search to words that are next to each other. For some searches this can greatly reduce the number of false hits that are returned. Not all databases use this standard. Check the help screens in a database or experiment with quotation marks to see if they function as a phrase limiter in a specific database.

Limit Search by Year Published

Many article databases go back many decades. Researchers are often looking for the most recent research on a topic, so limiting your search to the last few years in a database can be useful, especially if you are retrieving too many articles.

Limit Search by Language

Some large scholarly databases include articles in many different languages. Especially for topics relating to another country, such as "Mexican street gangs," it can be useful to limit your search to English if you cannot read other languages.

Limit Search by Publication Type

Some of the larger article databases that include journals, magazines, and other nonscholarly publications allow the searcher to limit to peer-review journals that have been vetted by other scholars during the publishing process. This usually involves checking a box for scholarly articles.

Many databases do not have the automatic capability of limiting a search to review articles only. Review articles are scholarly journal articles that provide a systematic review and critique of the research on a particular topic. They are valuable for the researcher because they point out weaknesses in earlier research, indicate areas where more research is needed, and pull together a large reference list of the important articles that have been written on a topic. Some databases have pull-down boxes that allow the researcher to select "review articles" and other databases can be tricked into searching for review articles by typing the word "review" or "annual review" (combined with keywords for your research topic) in the "journal" or "source" pull-down box.

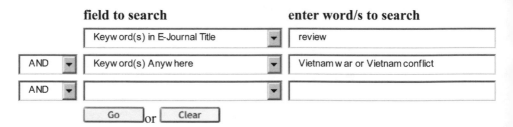

There are many other limits that can be set using specific article databases. History databases allow you to search by a specific historical time period, and law article databases let you search for articles focusing on a particular court case. Some databases also allow you to limit your search to book reviews or to journals held by your library.

LOCATE ARTICLES

The large majority of journal, magazine, and newspaper articles are not available for free on the web. Sometimes the current issue or parts of the most recent issue are available, but this is infrequently the case.

Academic libraries subscribe to thousands of online and print journals, magazines, and newspapers. At many libraries if you use the web from on campus or enter article databases via the library home page, you will be "authenticated" by the system as a member of your university community and you will be given free seamless access to many online articles. You may currently be using expensive sources without even being aware of it. Many libraries also provide off-campus access. See your own library home page for information about how best to access articles and databases from off-campus.

There are several ways to locate articles.

1. Use a full-text database. Many article databases, especially the large aggregators, are full-text and your search will retrieve the full text of the article.
2. Search an article database and click on the linking symbol for an individual article entry. Libraries use an OpenURL link resolver system such as SFX or LinkFinder Plus that provides a direct link from an article database to the journal or journal article you are seeking. This linking button is customized by your library and may be called "Get It" or "Find It" or similar language. The button is often customized with your institution name (e.g., "Get It at Cornell"). It will take you to either an online copy or the call number for the print version in the library.
3. Search an article database and then check the library catalog. If your library does not have a linking system in place, you need to make a note of the journal title, volume, and pages. Next, search the library online catalog to see if your library owns the journal and then link directly to the electronic copy or make a note of the call number so that you can locate it in the library.

Use interlibrary loan, also on your library web page, to borrow articles that your library does not own. Many article databases link directly to an interlibrary loan service through the SFX linking button.

USE OPEN ACCESS JOURNALS, PREPRINT SERVERS, AND INSTITUTIONAL REPOSITORIES/UNIVERSITY WEB SITES

Three trends in promoting scholarly research have recently been developed that seek to address problems with access, cost, and the timeliness with which academic research is published and shared.

Open Access journals are journals that are freely available over the web to all users. Copyright is usually retained by the author or institution that has a commitment to making research available to those who need it. The costs of publishing are thus shifted from the reader to the author or institution producing the research. Most Open Access journals are available by searching either a specialized discipline-specific journal database (see appendix) or one of the large multidisciplinary journal databases mentioned earlier in this chapter. Many Open Access journals go through the same scholarly peer-review process and editorial process as their counterparts in commercial or society publishing. Information on editorial policies is usually found on the journal web page.

Preprints are early versions of journal articles before they have gone through the peer-review and editorial processes in order to be formally published. The peer-review process can often take more than a year. For quickly moving fields, such as those in the sciences, preprint servers provide a place to get recently produced research. These articles must be more carefully evaluated than those that have undergone peer-review.

Preprint Servers

Multidisciplinary

arXiv e-Print Archive (Cornell University)
http://xxx.lanl.gov
Physics, mathematics, nonlinear science, computer science, and quantitative biology

E-Print Network (Department of Energy, Office of Scientific and Technical Information)
http://www.osti.gov/eprints
Physics, materials, chemistry, biology, environmental sciences, nuclear medicine

CogPrints: Cognitive Science E-Print Server (University of Southampton)
http://cogprints.soton.ac.uk
Psychology, neuroscience, linguistics, many areas of computer science, philosophy, biology, physical, social, and mathematical sciences that are pertinent to the study of cognition

Social Science Research Network
http://www.ssrn.com
Working papers in economics, finance, accounting, and law

Science Direct Preprint Archive
http://www.sciencedirect.com/preprintarchive
Mathematics, chemistry, computer science

Mathematics

Institute for Mathematical Sciences Preprint Server (Stony Brook University)
http://www.math.sunysb.edu/preprints.html

(continued)

Mathematical Physics Preprint Archives (University of Texas)
http://rene.ma.utexas.edu/mp_arc

Math Specialized Subject Server (American Mathematical Society)
http://www.ams.org/global-preprints/special-server.html

Physics

SPIRES (Stanford University)
http://www.slac.stanford.edu/spires/index.shtml

CERN Document Server
http://cds.cern.ch/

Chemistry

Chemistry Preprint Server
http://www.sciencedirect.com/preprintarchive

Biology & Ecology

BioMed Central
http://www.biomedcentral.com

Clinical Medicine Health Research NetPrints
http://clinmed.netprints.org

Ecology Preprint Registry (University of California at Santa Barbara)
http://www.nceas.ucsb.edu:8504/esa/ppr/ppr.Query

Institutional Repositories are university and other institutional web sites where research that has been produced by the institution has been compiled on the web and is usually free and searchable over the web. In a similar vein many faculty researchers post their scholarly work on their own home pages. Some of the larger institutional repositories include: *MIT DSPACE, University of California Escholarship Repository,* and *EPIC: Electronic Publishing Initiative at Columbia University.* Some research located in institutional repositories can be searched using OAIster (http://oaister.umdl.umich.edu) created by the University of Michigan. *Google Scholar* as well as other search engines provide access to some research located in institutional repositories.

EVALUATE ARTICLES

The bottom line in evaluating articles is to determine whether they are scholarly or popular. Use scholarly journal articles whenever possible. If there are no scholarly articles available yet because the topic is extremely current, use published newspaper or magazine articles rather than blogs or web pages.

Scholarly journal articles undergo a process of peer-review. This means that editors' decisions about whether or not to publish a paper are based on the judgments of experts, other scholars in the same field who review the manuscript prior to publication. Reviewers' comments serve to keep poorly constructed research out of journals and provide valuable feedback and corrections to authors who then make changes and improve the quality of the article being published. Some peer-review is "blind," meaning reviewers do not know the identity of the author they are reviewing so that the review will not be colored by any prior assumptions a reviewer might have about a particular author's work.

The following criteria will assist you in determining the scholarly value of an article.

Determine Purpose and Scholarly Nature

What is the purpose of the article? Was it written to further knowledge and research about a particular topic, or was it written to entertain or persuade? Determine the intended audience for the article. Was the article written for other scholars, educated laypeople, or for the general public? Determine if the article is a report on research findings or a secondhand report on research done by others.

Some clues for determining whether an article is scholarly include:

- the level and tone of the language,
- the length—scholarly articles can run ten to twenty pages,
- an extensive bibliography of reputable sources,
- an indication that research was conducted and conclusions were drawn—not a simple report of events,
- an author who is a professor or expert in the field,
- little, if any, advertising,
- an indication that a scholarly press, scholarly society, or academic institute published the article.

Evaluate Authority

Authority refers to the credentials of both the author and the publisher or sponsor of a journal, magazine, or newspaper. Scholarly journal articles often contain a sentence at the beginning or end of the article listing at minimum the author's institutional affiliation. Magazines sometimes provide a sentence about the credentials of the freelancer or journalist writing the article. Do a Google search to find the author's web page or check a journal database to see if the author has published other articles on the subject. Authors writing for scholarly journals are usually professors or experts in the field. Magazine and newspaper articles are written by journalists who write about many topics and typically do not have expertise in a particular area.

Find out the publisher of the journal, magazine, or newspaper article. If there is not a clear publisher listed, the article may be self-published on the web. This means it may not have gone through an editorial or peer-review process. A scholarly journal article can be published by a scholarly society or a commercial publisher. It will have an editor and editorial board of some sort, as well as an established submission and review procedure that is explained on the publisher's web site or at the front of a print copy of the journal.

Determine Possible Bias

Scholarly journal articles strive to present research that is accurate and free of bias. No article is completely objective, but the peer-review and editorial processes that scholarly publishers use filter out articles that do not adhere to good research standards and approved methodologies. Scholarly articles provide extensive bibliographies that link the work of one author to the research that has already been reported. No scholarly work is written in a vacuum—each article acknowledges how new research connects to earlier studies.

Many newspapers and magazines have a framework or belief system that influences what they print. A newspaper such as the *New York Times* has a strong commitment to objective and accurate reporting. The paper attempts to balance both conservative and liberal viewpoints on its editorial pages and also attempts to report on all sides of an issue. While some media watchdogs believe that the paper is not objective enough, a letters-to-the-editor section provides an outlet for opposing views. Thinking about the audience for a particular publication will assist you in determining if there is a strong agenda for that publication. A magazine such as *Working Mother* is not likely to publish an article arguing that mothers should stay out of the workforce.

Some publications such as *The Nation* (liberal) and *The National Review* (conservative) have long histories of publishing articles in support of a specific political agenda. This is not to say that the information reported in these articles is inaccurate, but only that it is important not to rely on one of these publications as your only support for drawing conclusions on a topic.

In some countries the major newspapers are directly tied to the government and reflect only government-supported positions on issues. Using a variety of news sources helps the researcher get a more balanced picture of an event.

Use Filters as Evaluation Tools

The following are filters you can use to limit your search to materials that are scholarly or more research-oriented. By using a good filter, much of the evaluative work is done for you—the filter identifies the higher quality titles on a topic.

- Use a specialized article database (see appendix) that covers scholarly journal articles and screens out popular magazine articles or any unpublished writings that have not been edited or fact-checked.
- Use bibliographies listed at the back of scholarly books, journal articles, or subject encyclopedias. The authors of these sources have provided authoritative screening for you by selecting key articles. A great deal of scholarly research is conducted by tracing the bibliographies of other researchers.
- Ask for recommendations from professors or other experts. Their years of knowledge and extensive reading provide a valuable human filter that can point to key resources.
- Use the *Web of Science*, a database that traces which journal articles are heavily cited by other researchers. *Google Scholar,* a new free service developed by Google, and *Scopus* are developing similar products, but currently they are significantly smaller than *Web of Science*.
- Use the "invisible college," a loosely defined network of scholars all working on similar research. The internet has made this "invisible college" of scholars more accessible to student researchers by opening up listservs, email, blogs, and conference proceedings to anyone who is interested. Through interactions with this network, important articles can be found.

Investigate Accuracy, Consistency, and Content

Determining accuracy involves viewing the article with a critical eye. Look for external consistency. Does the content seem to jibe with other research findings on the topic? Check also for internal consistency. Are the arguments that are being made supported within the work itself? Does the work seem plausible? Was the appropriate methodology used? Are statements backed up by citations to other research? Is the bibliography substantial and does it cite scholarly or popular sources?

If the article is a report on original research, examine whether the author provided a relevant and up-to-date literature review. Also determine whether the author has clearly stated a hypothesis, related the article to previous research, and interpreted the results correctly. Look for any discrepancies between the results and the hypothesis. Recent articles on assessing the quality of research can be found online (Greenhalgh 1997; Rumrill, Fitzgerald, and Ware 2000).

Note Currency

For some research the currency of an article is important. In some sciences, such as molecular biology or genetics, an article more than a year old can be too old to be useful. In the humanities, certain older articles are considered classics and are important to acknowledge in your research.

Determine Relevance

Decide whether the article directly relates to your research topic. Determine if the information in the article supports or refutes arguments you are trying to make. It is often tempting to include information that is interesting or exciting, but it may not further the goals of your research paper. When collecting resources to use for your paper, compare each source to the other sources you have gathered. Does one particular source add anything to the research you are presenting? What is the relative value of the source in question?

Examine Your Assumptions

Every researcher begins a project with some assumptions or hypotheses. It is important to put your own ideas aside as you gather and read articles on your topic. Ignoring articles that refute your hypothesis will not serve you in the long run. You must connect your ideas to previous research. Be open to adjusting your own set of beliefs about a topic as you digest the current research. It is acceptable to use articles to bolster your own arguments, but if there is substantial research out there that presents an alternative view, you must acknowledge and respond to it.

Use Multiple Sources

Whenever possible choose scholarly over popular articles and choose published articles over unpublished materials. For any argument you are making that is controversial, try to have more than one citation to an article that backs up your statements. If you can only find one article that supports your ideas, be suspicious—especially if the source is unpublished.

UNDERSTAND THE ROLE OF INFORMAL INFORMATION SOURCES: PERSONAL WEB PAGES, BLOGS, AND WIKIS

Over the past decade a variety of informal information sources have sprung up due to the convenience and accessibility of the web. These unpublished sources have their place in research, but should not be relied on as a primary means for gathering research to cite in your research paper.

Personal web pages are defined as self-published web pages that the writer of the page has put on the web rather than published resources that happen to be located on the web. The common thread is that these personal pages are unpublished and not fact-checked or edited in many cases. They can range from a professor's preprint unpublished article that is pretty reliable to the home page of your ten-year-old brother.

Blogs (weblogs) are web sites that contain periodic posts that are typically in reverse chronological order. They can be personal diaries, corporate information logs, or news and thoughts about a particular subject. They have one writer or a group of writers and sometimes provide space for public comments which can lead to a community of readers that are connected to the blog. A blog is usually run through a content management system. Blogs are not published in the traditional sense and only rarely will they have any editorial oversight or fact-checking.

A **wiki** is a collaborative web site comprised of the collective work of many authors. Wikis, named after the Hawaiian word wikiwiki, meaning "quick," are simple to use and edit. Frequently there is no review of edited pages and many wikis are open to the general public, usually without any registration procedures. Wikis are popular with scientists and software engineers, but they are starting to be used by many other people who are collaborating on projects. Wikis vary tremendously in their authoritativeness and reliability. The bottom line is that most entries on wikis are only as good as the last person who logged on to an entry and edited it. Even if a renowned expert wrote an entry, it could be subject to a child logging on and providing editorial assistance!

All of these informal communication mechanisms can be compared to other informal communications, including the following statements:

"My friend Jessica told me it was true."
"My dad has a friend at the research center who said they always do that."
"I heard a lecture by a famous scientist and he explained the theory this way . . ."

The quality of this information varies greatly. In the above examples, your friend, your dad, and the famous scientist may all be relaying correct information, but it is unfiltered and unpublished information that should not be cited in the bibliography of a research paper. Similarly, there is a great deal of information being produced through personal web pages, blogs, wikis, and other informal mechanisms. This information can be useful in providing ideas, examining controversies, and pointing to published sources. It is not reliable enough to cite in a quality research paper or article.

There are exceptions. A scholar might cite a scientist giving a lecture at a conference or even cite a conversation with a friend if the friend has expertise in a particular area. These exceptions are rare. If you are working on a very current event, you may need to cite something in a blog, but chances are you can find the same information in a newspaper that has been fact-checked. Typically, only scholars who have deep knowledge of a field can cite these informal modes of communication safely.

We are undergoing a rapid transformation in how information is produced and delivered. Once articles became available on the web, the need for strict evaluative criteria became paramount. Using published articles that have been through a review or, at minimum, an editorial process of some type is essential.

NOTES

1. Blogs, formally referred to as weblogs, are web pages that provide frequent short entries arranged in reverse chronological order about a specific topic or subject. They are written by a wide variety of people ranging from children to journalists.

2. For further information on the Open Access movement see: Guterman, Lila. 2004. The promise and peril of "open access." *Chronicle of Higher Education* 50, no. 21 (30 January): A10.

3. Some libraries use software to connect *Google Scholar* directly to the articles the library owns. If *Google Scholar* does not link to resources owned by your library, follow the steps on finding journal articles in this chapter so that you are not asked to pay for articles your library already owns.

REFERENCES

Greenhalgh, Trisha. 1997. How to read a paper: Assessing the methodological quality of published papers." *British Medical Journal* 315:305–308.

Rumrill, P., S. Fitzgerald, and M. Ware. 2000. Guidelines for evaluating research articles. *Work* 13, no. 3:257–263.

Weber, Thomas E. 2004. Blogs help you cope with data overload—If you manage them. *Wall Street Journal*, section B (8 July): 1.

4

Primary Sources: Online Tools and Digitized Collections

Research is the process of going up alleys to see if they are blind.

Marston Bates

The development of the web and the rapid digitization of many archival collections are transforming the climate for research using primary source collections. Though the majority of primary source documents remain available only in one location and in their original nondigitized format, hundreds of thousands of materials are now available on the web, providing an expansive collection for researchers to peruse. Tunneling into primary sources can be the most exciting part of research because it is through the use of these documents—some rarely viewed by another human since they were written—that creative and original research is produced.

Before tunneling in, it is important to consider what type of primary source you are seeking, and what the researchers who have gone before you have discovered. Secondary sources, such as journal articles and books, will keep you from "discovering" something in source documents that someone before you has already reported to the scholarly community. It is not possible to do original research until you are familiar with the work of scholars who have investigated similar terrain.

People have risked their lives rescuing primary source material from destruction, and people have spent their lives creating what we now define as primary sources. Primary sources are powerful and valuable.

In 1978, after the Soviet secret police began stealing manuscripts from noted nuclear scientist and Nobel Peace Prize winner Andrei Sakharov, he and his wife began smuggling his papers abroad. Taking considerable risks, friends often hid documents in their clothing in order to get them safely out of Russia. Today the Sakharov Archives are being scanned and made available over the Internet. (Bonner 1993)

When students in Iran seized the United States embassy in 1979 they acquired an enormous collection of classified U.S. documents, some intact, others improperly shredded so that the students were able to painstakingly piece them back together. By 1995, 77 volumes of "Documents from the U.S. Espionage Den" had been published in Iran. These original documents provide rich source material for scholars studying thirty years of United States involvement in Iran. The documents also illustrate the inner day-to-day workings of the CIA. At least one execution of a CIA source has been attributed to the capture of these records. (Epstein 1987)

Four of Walt Whitman's notebooks containing fragments and revisions of the poem "Song of Myself," as well as observations from the battlefield and in Civil War hospitals disappeared from the Library of Congress archives after they were packed away and stored outside of Washington D.C. during World War II. Surfacing at Sotheby's more than forty years later and carried by FBI escort to Washington, the notebooks, along with a missing hand colored paper butterfly belonging to Whitman, have been scanned onto the Internet for public viewing. A New York lawyer settling his father's estate had discovered the items. The fate of six still-missing notebooks is still unknown. (Library of Congress 2003)

WHAT ARE PRIMARY SOURCES?

> A primary source gives the words of the witnesses or the first recorders
> of an event.
>
> Helen J. Poulton, *The Historian's Handbook* (1972)

The concept of a "primary source" is elusive and its definition can vary by time and context and even by the type of scholar using it. To the historian, a primary source can be defined as the "words of the witnesses or the first recorders of an event." Today's newspaper article is not usually thought of as a primary source, but in twenty years historians can use it as a primary source. Primary sources consist of unpublished documents such as letters, diaries, minutes of meetings, government reports, tape recordings, and sketches, as well as sources such as books, magazines, and newspaper articles that were published during the time of the event or person being studied.

Perhaps the easiest way to explain the meaning of a "primary source" is to define what it is not: a primary source is not a secondary source. Secondary sources report on, analyze, summarize, or distill in some way information garnered from primary sources. They are derived from primary sources.

A biography of Thomas Jefferson is a secondary source based on information garnered from primary sources (interviews, diaries, eighteenth-century newspaper articles). Jefferson's own autobiography would be a primary source because he would be reporting firsthand knowledge of his life rather than relying on other documents. The research paper you write, using primary and other secondary sources, is a secondary source because it analyzes information from other sources.

Web pages can be either primary or secondary depending on their content and context. An eyewitness account of a fire in Chicago on the day it happened would be considered a primary source, though its authenticity might be difficult to determine if it comes from a personal web page rather than a reputable news organization such as CNN.

To social scientists primary sources can also consist of sets of raw data such as population statistics gathered by the U.S. Census or answers to a Gallup poll. To literature scholars a primary source can be the actual focus of study, such as the text of *The Color Purple* by Alice Walker. To a scientist, such as a biologist, the term "primary source" has a different meaning. Instead of being produced some time ago, a primary source in science is a report or article in a primary journal that is written by a person who has discovered new knowledge by making observations or conducting an experiment. It is *primary* because the researcher is reporting on new knowledge or original research rather than citing previous studies. This chapter will cover primary sources of interest to historians and those in related fields.

UNDERSTAND THE TYPES OF PRIMARY SOURCES

There are many types of and formats for primary sources. Sometimes the types of resources overlap: for example, an original photograph might be available in the special collections area of a library, on the web, or reproduced in a book. The types of primary sources you use for your research will depend on what your topic is, what is available within your own library or on the web, and whether or not you are able to visit other libraries or repositories. For undergraduate research it is not uncommon to first locate an exciting primary source collection and then develop or revise a research topic to fit the collection available.

There are two large categories of primary source materials: unpublished documents such as archival or manuscript collections, and published or reprinted texts.

Unpublished Sources: Archives and Manuscripts

Archives are defined as collections of documents and records from organizations, which can include the papers of those associated with the organization. Manuscripts are collections of personal unpublished papers and correspondence relating to or written by an individual. These unpublished primary source materials can range from musical notes written on a napkin by a composer, who jots down the first few bars of a soon-to-be famous musical to the complete records of an organization such as the correspondence memos, and meeting minutes of the Students for a Democratic Society. Even email, such as the forty million email messages archived after eight years of the Clinton administration, including correspondence with White House aide Monica Lewinsky is now considered primary source material available for study by historians.

Unpublished sources are more difficult to find than published sources, but they can provide new and intriguing information about a topic or person. The original creator of the document, letter, or diary often did not intend for the contents to be made public. These unique items stored in vast collections in library archives and special collections are an unlimited resource for future historians.

Archives differ from published books and articles in that they are discrete pieces of information such as letters, business cards, or ledgers. Though unpublished, archival information is organized into collections based on the principles of provenance and original order. An isolated letter by itself often has little meaning because it lacks a context. To maintain the intellectual meaning of primary sources, record groups are formed in order to pull together items created by the same office, organization, or person. The principle of original order involves keeping records organized in a meaningful way that relates to when these records were created or how they were used rather than establishing an arbitrary numbering system. This context, often provided by finding aids, gives researchers information about how records were created and organized, and also provides contextual meaning and value.

Published Texts

Primary sources can be published texts in two different ways. Original documents can be reproduced or reprinted in an article or book such as *The Letters of a Civil War Surgeon*. This book reproduces original letters written in the 1860s that have been collected and edited by a university professor into a newly published volume. Or, the book or article could be the actual published or printed work that appeared during the time period you are studying. For example, *The Young Girl's Book of Healthful Amusements and Exercises* is a book published in 1840 about physical education for girls.

Newspaper articles, magazine or other serially produced articles, books (both fiction and nonfiction), and government documents are all common types of primary sources that researchers use. They are usually easier to find than unpublished materials because there are many indexes and databases that provide access to them. They are frequently owned by libraries either in their original format or reproduced on microform, or they may be digitized and available over the web. Many types of primary sources can be found in published materials, including facsimiles (exact copies) of advertisements, maps, pamphlets, and posters.

Magazine and newspaper articles provide the most immediate reactions to historical events from those closely connected to the events. Government documents are also useful for certain topics and are widely available in microform, print, and online through many libraries and government repositories. Government documents can also include unpublished correspondence and papers that have been archived though they were not originally made available to the public. These papers can provide fascinating insights into the thought processes of those creating public policy. Government documents also include the documents of international bodies such as the United Nations. Many historians view government documents as the most useful type of primary source because although they are not without bias, they provide a reliable record of what occurred during a particular time.

Older published or printed historical materials are sometimes gathered into large collections such as the *American Periodical Series*, which includes over one thousand magazines published between 1741 and 1900, including *Benjamin Franklin's General Magazine* and early editions of *Ladies' Home Journal*.

Other Types of Primary Sources

Primary sources are not confined to the written word. They can also include the following.

Oral histories, such as the *Holocaust Survivors Oral History Project*, provide access to the experiences of ordinary people who lived through an event or a particular historical time period. These histories can be on tape, online, or transcribed into print. Oral histories of members of minority groups are especially useful for tapping into experiences not captured by mainstream publishing. The *Directory of Oral History Collections* provides information about collections available around the country. *History-Makers*, a digital collection of videotaped interviews with more than five thousand prominent African Americans, is in the process of being recorded and compiled for future historians studying African Americans' contributions to the twentieth century. (For more information on oral history research, see chapter 5.)

Visual and audio documents such as films, photographs, maps, artwork, and songs provide evidence about a specific moment in history. They can provide researchers with information about culture, customs, styles, and life experiences that text does not convey. The Library of Congress "Save Our Sounds" project has preserved historically important sounds such as Martin Luther King Jr. giving his "I Have a Dream" speech and Woody Guthrie singing "This Land Is Your Land." The Smithsonian Institution has digitized numerous photographs, including images of items left at the Vietnam War Memorial and advertisements (broadsides) for nineteenth-century "magic lantern" early cinema shows.

Machine readable data sets, frequently available over the internet, are collections of numeric data that can be analyzed and manipulated to provide answers to research questions. The Inter-University Consortium for Political and Social Research, the largest repository of collections of data in the United States, includes data on drug use, elections, aging, and education, as well as other social and political issues.

Realia or artifacts include architectural blueprints, clothing, jewelry, needlework, scrapbooks, postcards, and other types of objects. These objects are often used in exhibits and museums. The *American Memory Project* at the Library of Congress has digitized pictures of thousands of artifacts, including Harry Houdini's handcuffs from 1900, and Bob Hope's business card from 1920.

PLAN YOUR RESEARCH STRATEGY

Research using primary sources is time consuming. Like digging for a needle in a haystack, the researcher often needs to sift through a large quantity of information before finding something useful. There are several steps to conducting primary source research that are elaborated below.

Research Secondary Sources First

Your success in pursuing primary source material will depend on your understanding and knowledge of the secondary literature—the information on your topic found in books, journal articles, and encyclopedias.

Secondary sources will help you hone in on your topic. What are the parameters of your research? If your topic is witchcraft, will you focus on the present day or a particular historical period and country? Are you interested in the Salem witch trials, and if so, are you interested in how this historical time was reflected in American literature, or are you interested in the psychological aspects of this event? As you investigate your subject you will discover what ground other researchers have covered and what still needs to be pursued. Return frequently to the secondary literature even after you have started searching primary source collections.

These books and articles will help you evaluate your source material and keep in touch with key research and theories that have been developed on your subject.

Secondary articles and books have the added advantage of connecting you quickly and directly with primary source collections. Rather than reinventing the wheel, the best way to locate primary sources is to piggyback onto someone who has gone before you. If you are researching the life of Margaret Sanger and you read the secondary literature about her—biographies, journal articles, and history books on the birth control movement—the researchers will list in their bibliographies some of the primary sources they used. If Sanger's archives are collected and housed at a particular library, reprinted in a book, or digitized on the web, that information will be available to you without your having to track it down.

Make a List of Key People, Dates, and Terms

Many archive and manuscript collections, as well as indexes to older newspaper and magazine articles, are organized by names, dates, places, and events. Having the correct spelling and accurate dates will allow you to do your research efficiently. Use a subject encyclopedia to identify important places, people, and events. Some subject encyclopedias will also lead you to the major archival collections that cover your topic. If you are researching a person, find out their organizational affiliations and whether they associated with well-known people from the time period. Books and journal articles will give you background information about your topic and may also cite primary source documents that their investigators used for their research. (For more information about finding books and articles, see chapters 2 and 3.)

Determine What Type of Primary Source to Use

Your research goals need to be limited by the amount of time you have and your geographic mobility. In the past it was uncommon for inexperienced researchers to use primary source materials because of time and travel expenses. Today primary sources are more accessible because more resources are being digitized and made available over the web. Primary sources are also more frequently reproduced in books, and large collections of primary sources are available in microform collections owned by many college and research libraries.

Use the following criteria to determine which of the sections to pursue in this chapter:

- Find Digitized Primary Source Collections on the Web

  - This section is best used if you are researching a well-known person or topic that is likely to have been digitized or if you have some flexibility in the topic you choose. Though many primary sources have been digitized, the vast majority remain in their original form or in microform.

- Find Primary Sources Using the Online Library Catalog

  - This section is useful if you are looking for well-known people, historical events, or groups of people (Black Panthers, Asian immigrants), and if it is likely that the papers, letters, or other documents have been reprinted or published in some form.

- Visit Your Special Collections Department

  - Choosing this section largely depends on what is housed in your library's special collections departments. Locate that department on the web page to review the depth of its collections.

- Find Historical Newspaper and Magazine Articles

  - This section offers one of the easiest ways to gather primary source material about a person or event. Many full-text collections of articles now exist for historical research.

- Use Special Microform Collections of Primary Sources

  - Choose this section for older historical materials such as published books, newspapers, and broadsides.

Using *published* sources such as older newspaper and magazine articles will be easy to accomplish in most academic, research, and large public libraries. Finding a particular person's diaries or papers might involve logging onto the web, but more frequently could entail traveling across the country to the repository that houses those manuscripts. One alternative, depending on the parameters of your research assignment, is to find a primary source collection that intrigues you and then develop a research project that relates to that collection (if your professor allows you that leeway).

FIND DIGITIZED PRIMARY SOURCE COLLECTIONS ON THE WEB

Tens of thousands of archival collections can be found on the web. These digitized primary sources provide researchers with unprecedented access to collections that previously were only available in one location and kept behind locked doors. Information about many more archival collections is available on the web. This information indicates what is owned by a particular archive and provides search aids that give a detailed inventory of the holdings of a particular collection and other descriptive information. There remain many complex technical, legal, and monetary problems involved in scanning primary sources. Many archival collections remain in their original format and are available in only one physical location.

The following sections list some of the larger digital library collections on the web, followed by archival search engines and finding tools that point to digitized and traditional print collections. There is also a section on collections outside of the United States. If you have some flexibility with the topic you are working on you might want to browse one of the larger collections such as the *American Memory Project*. Locate an interesting collection and work backward to the development of your topic. If your topic is already fixed, try the archival search engines listed below.

Use Large Digital Library Collections to Find Primary Sources

The American Memory Project (Library of Congress)
http://memory.loc.gov/ammem/ammemhome.html
This web site provides access to archives throughout the United States in a wide variety of subjects such as the Woman Suffrage Movement, American Life Histories from the Federal Writers' Project, Baseball Highlights (1860s to the 1960s), and many other American history topics.

ARC: Archival Research Catalog (National Archives and Records Administration)
http://www.archives.gov/research_room/arc/
ARC contains descriptions of the National Archives' collections, including films, still pictures, texts, and drawings, as well as digitized images of thousands of these items.

CIS History Universe (LexisNexis)
CIS is a collection of selected primary and secondary sources in African American Studies and Women's Studies. Included are the full text of laws and court cases, autobiographies, and manuscripts. (Library subscription required.)

Electronic Text Center (University of Virginia Library)
http://etext.lib.virginia.edu/uvaonline.html
This extensive digitized collection includes more than 70,000 humanities texts in thirteen languages, 350,000 images including manuscripts, newspaper pages, and page images of special collections books. Though this is one of the larger collections, many college and university libraries are building similar types of digitized repositories.

Library and Archival Exhibitions on the Web (Smithsonian Institute)
http://www.sil.si.edu/SILPublications/Online-Exhibitions/
This web site provides links to online exhibits created by libraries and archival repositories. Most of the collections focus on images of printed books, book illustrations, manuscripts, photographs, posters, and archival audio and video.

The Making of America (University of Michigan and Cornell University)
http://www.hti.umich.edu/m/moagrp/
MOA contains millions of pages from more than thirteen thousand volumes of primary source materials owned by the University of Michigan and Cornell University. The focus of *MOA* is the nineteenth century and the collection contains journal articles and books in the areas of agriculture, education, psychology, American history, sociology, religion, science, and technology.

United States Historical Census Data Browser (University of Virginia Libraries)
http://fisher.lib.virginia.edu/collections/stats/histcensus/
Hosted by the University of Virginia Libraries, this site provides data from the United States Decennial Census describing the people and economy of each state from 1790 to 1960.

Use Archive Search Engines to Find Digitized Collections

The original purpose of many of the sites below has been to compile a listing of specific collections with information about where they are held. As finding aids and collections have become digitized, these tools have added links to resources as they become available over the web.

American and British History Sources on the Internet (Rutgers University Libraries)
http://www.libraries.rutgers.edu/rul/rr_gateway/research_guides/history/history.shtml
This Rutgers-sponsored web site provides an extensive index with links to historical resources.

Archives USA (Proquest/UMI)
Archives USA is an online catalog of more than 130,000 collections. The purpose of this resource is to locate archival collections in the United States. In some cases there are also links to online finding aids and digitized collections. *Archives USA* integrates three resources: the *National Union Catalog of Manuscript Collections (NUCMC)*, the *Directory of Archives and Manuscript Repositories in the United States (DARMUS)*, and the *National Inventory of Documentary Sources in the United States (NIDS)*. (Library subscription required.)

The Avalon Project (Yale University)
http://www.yale.edu/lawweb/avalon/avalon.htm

The Avalon Project provides digitized documents with links to supporting documents in the fields of law, history, economics, politics, diplomacy, and government.

Eureka/RedLightGreen (Research Libraries Group)
http://www.redlightgreen.com
Eureka includes the holdings of about 150 major research libraries, archives, and museums in the United States, as well as some materials from other countries. *RedLightGreen* is a version of the catalog that is free to the public. In *Eureka*, use the "limit" command to restrict your search to archival collections.

A Geographic Guide to Uncovering Women's History in Archival Collections (University of Texas)
http://www.lib.utsa.edu/Archives/WomenGender/links.html
This web site provides a geographical listing by state of archival collections relating to the history of women in the United States. This is an example of the type of site that some college and university libraries are providing to bring together archival collections on a particular subject area. *Women and Social Movements in the United States*, subscribed to by some libraries, is also a good resource for accessing electronic archives on women in the United States from 1600 to 1900.

National Union Catalog of Manuscript Collections (NUCMC) (Library of Congress)
http://www.loc.gov/coll/nucmc/nucmc.html
NUCMC indexes more than 700,000 records of archival and manuscript collections in research libraries, museums, state archives, and historical societies located throughout North America. The information provided is usually limited to what institution houses a particular collection, but links to digitized collections are provided when available.

Ready, Net, Go! (Tulane University)
http://www.tulane.edu/~miller/ArchivesResources.html
This web site is really an "index of indexes" to archive collections. It is especially useful for international archival resources.

Repositories of Primary Sources in the U.S. (University of Idaho)
http://www.uidaho.edu/special-collections/Other.Repositories.html
This web site links to thousands of collections in the United States. Some are links to web pages that discuss collections and others are actual digitized collections. The site is organized by region and state.

RLG Archival Resources (Research Libraries Group)
http://www.rlg.org/arr
Archival Resources, compiled by the Research Libraries Group, is a large database subscribed to by some research libraries. It contains finding aids for archival col-

lections. In some cases the finding aids link directly to digitized collections. It is available at some research libraries.

RLG Cultural Materials (Research Libraries Group)
http://culturalmaterials.rlg.org/
RLG Cultural Materials is a database containing integrated descriptions and digital representations (images, texts, sound, and motion) of cultural objects from research collections in libraries, archives, historical societies, and museums. It is available at some research libraries.

State Archive Collections (Georgia Secretary of State Office)
http://www.sos.state.ga.us/archives/
The Office of the Secretary of State of Georgia has compiled a list of links to state archival collections as well as other useful resources for archives research.

WorldCat (OCLC)
WorldCat contains the records listed in most library catalogs throughout the United States and some library catalogs from a few other countries as well. *WorldCat* can sometimes be the best place to find corporate archives, church records, and historical society records, as well as other archival materials. In the advanced search mode, limit your format to "archival materials." (Library subscription required.)

Use Indexes and Archive Search Engines to Find Archives in Other Countries

Africa Research Central (California State University Library, San Bernadino)
http://www.africa-research.org/

Archon (Royal Commission on Historical Manuscripts)
http://www.archon.nationalarchives.gov.uk/archon

CAIN: Canadian Archival Information Network (Canadian Council of Archives)
http://www.cain-rcia.ca/cain/e_home.html

EAN: European Archival Network (Swiss Federal Archives)
http://www.european-archival.net/

EuroDocs (Brigham Young University)
http://library.byu.edu/~rdh/eurodocs/

New Zealand National Register of Archives and Manuscripts (National Library of New Zealand cooperative venture)
http://www.nram.org.nz/

Register of Australian Archives and Manuscripts (National Library of Australia)
http://www.nla.gov.au/raam/

UNESCO Archives Portal (United Nations)
http://www.unesco.org/webworld/portal_archives/pages/Archives/

Most special collections are not in digitized form, but many can at least be located using the tools mentioned above. Some collections, however, can only be located by using print directories.[1]

FIND PRIMARY SOURCES USING THE ONLINE LIBRARY CATALOG

Your library's online catalog provides access to many primary source materials owned by the library, especially those that have been reprinted or published. The catalog can be found on the main library web page. Primary sources collected in larger microform collections or special collections housed at your library may or may not be in the library catalog, depending on the library's practices. Do not assume that by using the online catalog you are gaining access to *all* the primary source material owned by your library.

Autobiographies, collections of letters, reprinted diaries or diary entries, photographs, and many other resources are available through the online catalog simply by combining your topic as a keyword search with one of the following subject headings (or several of them strung together with the word "or" between each term). These terms can be entered in the "subject" field of your online catalog. "Sources" tends to be one of the most common subject headings used for primary source materials in library catalogs.

sources	personal narratives
correspondence	diaries
interviews	pamphlets
documents	documents
letters	interviews
speeches	quotations
manuscripts	reports

If you were researching nurses who served in the Vietnam War, you might try the following:

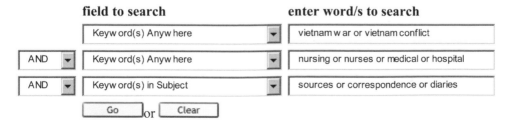

Another way to search for primary sources in the catalog is by author or "corporate" author. For example:

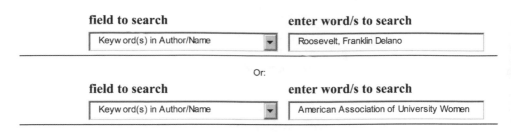

field to search	enter word/s to search
Keyword(s) in Author/Name ▼	Roosevelt, Franklin Delano

Or:

field to search	enter word/s to search
Keyword(s) in Author/Name ▼	American Association of University Women

In addition, it can be useful to search the online catalog for contextual materials, books published contemporaneously with the event or person you are studying. Most online library catalogs allow you to limit by date range without entering a particular subject.

Another resource commonly used is *Cumulative Book Index*. Owned by most libraries, this resource provides a chronological list of books published from 1908 to the present. For books published in the United States, the following two resources list books published between 1639 and 1845:

Charles Evans. 1941. *American Bibliography: A Chronological Dictionary of all Books, Pamphlets, and Periodical Publications Printed in the United States of America from the Genesis of Printing in 1639 Down to and Including the Year 1820.* New York: P. Smith.

Ralph R. Shaw and Richard H. Shoemaker. 1958. *American Bibliography: A Preliminary Checklist (1801–1819).* New York: Scarecrow Press.

For other countries, national bibliographies (lists of books) are published and can be located by using the British Library web site (http://www.bl.uk/collections/wider/natbibs.html) or the book *An Annotated Guide to Current National Bibliographies* compiled by Barbara Bell (1986. Alexandria, VA: Chadwyck-Healey).

VISIT YOUR SPECIAL COLLECTIONS DEPARTMENT

Most academic libraries have archival or manuscript collections in a separate area of the library sometimes called the special collections department. There are several ways to access materials in the special collections area of a library.

- Many online library catalogs provide access to at least some of the special collections housed in your library. Use the "limit" feature of the catalog to search for only archives and manuscripts.

- Find the web page for your library's special collections department. It is usually linked from the main library web page. Get an overview of the types of materials housed in your library. In some cases you will be able to view online finding aids and guides before you visit the collection.
- Visit your special collections department by planning ahead. Many archivists prefer that you make an appointment and in some cases notify them as to what you will be seeking when you arrive.

Archival research is often a multistep process. First you must identify a particular collection you want to study. Next you must determine if there is a finding aid for the collection. A finding aid is a detailed description of the contents of a particular collection. It is sometimes called a register or inventory and includes a description of each box or folder within a collection. Only after spending time with the finding aid will you be able to identify the particular parts of the collection you wish to study. Collections are usually arranged in the order that their creator imposed upon them so that the topic you are investigating may not be pulled together in one part of the finding aid. Once you have identified items in the collection that you need, the Special Collections librarian or archivist will retrieve the material.

FIND HISTORICAL NEWSPAPER AND MAGAZINE ARTICLES

Newspaper and magazine articles can provide fascinating accounts of a particular historical event or person. Searching for these articles has become much easier with the advent of online full-text databases. These databases are still a long way from providing a complete historical record, but they do provide access to a number of influential titles. If additional articles are needed, online indexes provide access to articles from other titles that must then be tracked down in print or microform using the library online catalog.

For those doing extensive research, or research on a somewhat obscure topic, using print indexes and special subject bibliographies will be necessary. For example, research on reactions to Martin Luther King Jr.'s "I Have a Dream" speech can be conducted by searching the full text of the *New York Times*, whereas research on the Native American reaction to the Battle of Little Bighorn might require consulting a special subject bibliography such as *American Indian and Alaska Native Newspapers and Periodicals, 1826–1924*, and then scanning dozens of magazines and newspapers covering the relevant dates of the event.

Use a Full-Text Database

Ideally the full text of *all* older newspapers and magazines would be available electronically. Though this is far from the case, there are a number of recently developed full-text databases that provide access to a range of historical newspapers and magazines. The following is a list of these collections. They all allow keyword searching by subject, author, and title, and in some cases the full text of the article can be searched. Use synonyms connected by "or" or try several different searches in order to do a comprehensive search. Remember to use the language of the time period being studied. A search for "African Americans" in a nineteenth-century newspaper database will not yield any results; instead, use terms such as Negro or Negroes.

The following collections have the full text of newspapers and magazines available online. A URL is given for those that are free over the web; others may be available from your library web page under "Full-Text Databases," "Electronic Databases," "Online Resources," or a similar phrase.

Accessible Archives is a collection of full-text newspapers and magazines including *Godey's Lady's Book* from 1830 to 1880, African American newspapers from the nineteenth century, and newspapers from the Civil War. (Library subscription required.)

American Periodicals Series (APS Online) covers magazines from 1740 to 1805, but eventually will include magazines through 1900. (Library subscription required.)

British Library Online Newspaper Archive (http://www.uk.olivesoftware.com/) includes selected facsimile issues of the *Daily News, Manchester Guardian, News of the World,* and *Weekly Dispatch* for scattered years from 1851 to 1918.

The Gerritsen Collection contains the full text of more than 4,700 publications, including newspapers and magazines from Europe, the United States, Canada, and New Zealand, dating from 1543 to 1945. The collection focuses on articles relating to the condition of women during this time period. (Library subscription required.)

Historical Newspapers: Palmer's Full Text Online, 1785–1870, contains articles from the *Times* of London from 1785 to 1980. (Library subscription required.)

Internet Library of Early Journals (http://www.bodley.ox.ac.uk/ilej/) includes digitized issues of six British magazines from the eighteenth and nineteenth centuries.

JSTOR includes the full text of older issues of more than one hundred scholarly journals from different disciplines. Many of the titles begin in the 1800s and continue until the most recent two to five years. (Library subscription required.)

Making of America (http://moa.umdl.umich.edu/index.html) is a digitized collection of more than fifty thousand journal articles and thousands of full-text books dating from the nineteenth century. (Library subscription required.)

The Nation Digital Archive contains the full text of *The Nation*, a liberal political magazine. Full text is available from 1865 to 1999. (Library subscription required.)

Proquest Historical Newspapers contains the full text of the *New York Times* (1851–1999), the *Wall Street Journal* (1889–1985), the *Chicago Tribune* (1890–1946), the *Christian Science Monitor* (1908–1990), and the *Los Angeles Times* (1881–1984). (Library subscription required.)

Times Literary Supplement (TLS) Centenary Archive includes the full text of reviews, letters, poems, and articles appearing in this publication from 1902 to 1990. (Library subscription required.)

U.S. News Archives on the Web (http://www.ibiblio.org/slanews/internet/archives.html) compiled by the Special Libraries Association provides links to newspapers available on the web, some for a fee and others for free.

Use an Online Newspaper or Magazine Index

If a newspaper or magazine article is not available in full text online, the next step is to find an online index that covers newspapers and magazines from the place and time period that you are studying. Though some libraries now have direct links from the index to the library catalog, the process of retrieving the article will typically consist of two steps:

1. Locate the article in the online index and make a note of the title, date, and page number.
2. Search your library online catalog for the actual newspaper or magazine title.

If your library does not own the title, you can borrow older newspapers or magazines, usually on microfilm, through the interlibrary loan department of your library. The following are online indexes to popular newspapers and magazines.

Alternative Press Index covers citations to articles from alternative, leftist, and radical magazines and newspapers from 1969 to the present. From 1991 to the present, this index is available online.

Foreign Broadcast Information Service (FBIS) Electronic Index covers translations of broadcasts, news agency transmissions, newspapers, magazines, and other sources of information from around the world from 1975 to 1996. The full text of these translations from 1996 to the present is available through the database *World News Connection.*

Index to Early American Periodicals covers all known periodical publications running between 1741 and 1935. The actual periodicals are on microfilm in the collection *American Periodicals Series.* This index is available only in print in some libraries.

International Index to Black Periodicals indexes over 150 scholarly and popular journals and magazines from the United States, Africa, and the Caribbean. Most articles are from the past five years, but some titles go back more than fifty years. Some articles are available in full text online.

Nineteenth-Century Masterfile (Poole's Plus) indexes nineteenth-century American and British magazines and newspapers and some government documents.

PCI WEB (Periodicals Contents Index) indexes the tables of contents of thousands of magazines and journals from their first issues (some start in the 1700s) to the early 1990s. Titles are from North America, the United Kingdom, Ireland, France, and Germany.

Reader's Guide Abstracts (1983–present) and *Reader's Guide Retrospective* (1963–1982) are online indexes to hundreds of popular U.S. and Canadian magazines.

Use a Print Newspaper or Magazine Index

If your library does not subscribe to online full-text articles or indexes to historical newspaper and magazine collections, print indexes are available in many libraries. Some examples are: *Index to Early American Periodicals, Poole's Index to Periodical Literature, Readers' Guide to Periodical Literature*, and *The New York Times Index*. Also, the Library of Congress provides links to local newspaper indexes or information about them at http://www.loc.gov/rr/news/oltitles.html. Many local papers provide full-text newspaper archives online going back between two and ten years. Sometimes local papers and indexes are available at the local public library.

Find a Specific Type of Newspaper

Sometimes you need to track down newspapers from a particular geographic location, like newspapers available in Georgia during the Civil War. And sometimes you need to find a newspaper or magazine that represents the views of a particular group, such as African Americans, during a particular historical period. The online library catalog can be searched for these types of newspapers. For example:

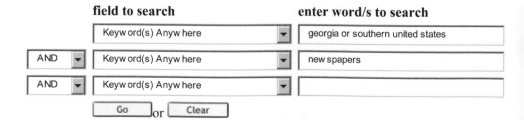

Or, for example:

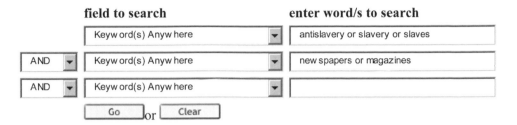

field to search		enter word/s to search
	Keyword(s) Anywhere ▾	antislavery or slavery or slaves
AND ▾	Keyword(s) Anywhere ▾	newspapers or magazines
AND ▾	Keyword(s) Anywhere ▾	
	Go or Clear	

There are many specialized books such as the *Directory of Ethnic Newspapers and Periodicals in the United States, African-American Newspapers and Periodicals*, and *Women's Periodicals in the United States* that can also be used to locate particular types of newspapers or magazines.

USE SPECIAL MICROFORM COLLECTIONS OF PRIMARY SOURCES

Many research libraries own primary source collections on microfiche or microfilm. These collections are sometimes indexed in the library online catalog. They range from the records of a particular organization such as the *Papers of the Association of Southern Women for the Prevention of Lynching* to enormous collections containing older books and newspapers from a particular time period.

The following is a selective list of some of the larger collections available. Consult a reference librarian for assistance finding a collection that might cover your area of interest or search the online library catalog by topic and limit your search to "microform."

American Culture Series (books and pamphlets published prior to 1875)

Early American Imprints (books, broadsides, and pamphlets printed between 1639 and 1819; available online in some libraries)

Early American Newspapers (newspapers published in the United States between 1704 and 1820; available online in some libraries)

Columbia University Oral History Project (interviews with political figures, authors, business leaders, and other important figures in twentieth-century American history)

CRITICALLY EVALUATE PRIMARY SOURCES

Critically evaluating primary sources is the responsibility of the researcher using the source. Unlike published sources, the only possible filtering or vetting process that has occurred with a primary source is that a special collections or archives department has made a choice to retain a particular item. Specific strategies need to be employed that are unique to primary source research. Working with primary sources is like detective work—leads must be followed, motives evaluated, and stories matched for consistency. The following strategies, typically employed by historians, need to be used to carefully analyze the sources you choose to include in your research. Evaluative criteria vary from one discipline to another and from one research project to another—this is not a comprehensive list.

Creator Bias

Every primary source has a creator and every creator has a point of view or bias. The bias in a source does not render it useless, but must be factored in when evaluating the information contained in a source. A photograph, for example, even before the days of computerized airbrushing, is influenced by the bias of the creator. Settings can be manipulated or the photographer can choose to take some pictures of an event and not others.

When reading or viewing a primary source it is important to consider who the creator was and what their relationship was to the event or situation being recorded.

1. What was the creator's view or purpose?
2. What did the creator include and not include in his or her reporting?
3. Was the source created on the spur of the moment or was more thought put into its creation?
4. Did the creator see the event firsthand or did he or she report on what others related?
5. Did the creator have a special interest in the event, or was he or she neutral?
6. Was the creator producing something for his or her personal use, for a friend, or for the public?
7. Is the language of the creator neutral or persuasive?

Read critically and skeptically. Though some primary sources are believed to be more reliable than others, every source contains some weakness or bias. Think carefully about the social, political, and economic contexts in which a source may have been created.

Time and Place

Historians use the "time and place" rule to evaluate the quality of a primary source. The closer in time and place a source and its creator were to an event, the better the chances are that the source is valid. A firsthand observer who witnessed a Civil War battle and wrote a letter about it will have more worth as a primary source than an account written by someone who was not a witness and relied on accounts from others.

Internal Consistency

Read your source document for internal consistency. Think like an interrogator working with a criminal suspect. Does the creator of your document stick to the same story? Are there reasons why the creator might not be completely honest in his or her report? If it is an oral history, are there reasons why the person being interviewed might not be telling the whole truth to the interviewer?

External Consistency

Compare the account you are reading to other primary sources produced in that time period. If you are reading someone's letters, you might want to compare the letters to an autobiography or newspaper article published during the same time period to see if it gives a similar account. Do not assume that one type of document, such as a published newspaper, is more reliable than a letter. The newspaper reporter may have a particular agenda or bias that the letter writer did not. Compare your source with secondary sources and other facts and data compiled about that time period. It is especially important to be up to date in your reading of secondary literature, including current books and journal articles that cover the topic or person under study.

Omissions

Be aware of what a creator chose to omit from his or her record about an event or person, as well as what the creator chose to include. Were significant facts or important issues left out of the writings? Or did the creator come into contact with only a certain segment of the population and only report the views of a particular group?

Selectivity

With a wealth of resources available, it is essential to be selective in the choices you make as to which sources to include in your research. Choose materials that pertain directly to your research question and that seem reliable. Do not choose resources that seem exciting if they are not directly related to your research. Sometimes it is tempting to include too much in your research paper because it is interesting or because you feel that it is worth including since you tracked it down and read it. Avoid having a research paper that becomes what William Storey calls a "garbage disposal" of information instead of a focused paper (Storey 1999).

Researcher Bias

Do not read into your sources what is not there. If your sources do not support your thesis, then you must adjust your thesis or track down additional sources to see if there is credible support for your ideas. Be aware of how your set of values might differ from the creator's value system. You are not neutral. You should not interpret the creator's writing in light of your own values, but with knowledge about the creator's value system. Come up with multiple interpretations of the text and explore the cultural and psychological undertones in the text. Be open to recognizing patterns that emerge in the primary sources you are studying. If these patterns do not match your own ideas, be willing to shift your ideas. Again, always check in with the secondary literature, journal articles, and books, to see what previous researchers concluded.

Multiple Sources

Do not rely on one set of papers from a single entity. One hundred years from now if you use the papers and manuscripts of the Catholic Church to determine general public views about same-sex marriages, the papers would not reflect the beliefs held by a large percentage of the population.

An Ongoing Process

Critical evaluation needs to be embedded in every step when conducting research using primary sources. Determining and revising your research question, choosing your tools and source materials, and comparing your results with other source materials and secondary literature are all essential components of the research process. In most other types of research, filtering and vetting have already been applied to the materials under study—journal articles have been reviewed and evaluated for content, books have been approved for publishing by editors. When using primary sources, you take on the role of reviewer and ultimately determine which sources can be trusted and verified and which sources need to be handled with more skepticism.

NOTES

1. The following print directories can be useful for locating difficult-to-find primary sources.

Directory of Archives and Manuscript Repositories in the United States (1988). Phoenix, AZ: Oryx Press.

DeWitt, Donald L. (1994). *Guides to Archives and Manuscript Collections in the United States.* Westport, CT: Greenwood Press.

Library of Congress (ongoing). *The National Inventory of Documentary Sources in the United States*, NIDS. Teaneck, NJ: Chadwyck-Healey.

Ash, Lee, and William G. Miller (1993). *Subject Collections: A Guide to Special Book Collections and Subject Emphases as Reported by University, College, Public, and Special Libraries and Museums in the United States and Canada.* New Providence, NJ: R.R. Bowker.

REFERENCES

Bonner, Elena. 1993. Presentation at Sakharov Archives Dedication Ceremony, July. http://www.brandeis.edu/departments/sakharov/index.html. Accessed December 2, 2003.

Epstein, Edward Jay. 1987. Secrets from the CIA archive in Teheran. *Orbis* 31:33–41.

Library of Congress. *American memory project.* http://memory.loc.gov/ammem/wwhtml/wwhome.html. Accessed December 2, 2003.

Poulton, Helen J. 1972. *The historian's handbook.* Norman: University of Oklahoma Press. 175–176.

Storey, William Kelleher. 1999. *Writing history: A guide for students.* New York; Oxford: Oxford University Press.

5

Biographical Research

Biography lends to death a new terror.

Oscar Wilde

Biographical writing dates back to ancient times, but it became widespread during the eighteenth century. Frequently relied on by historians, life writing—encompassing both autobiographical and biographical writing—is now being explored in many other disciplines, including literary criticism, anthropology, sociology, psychology, theology, and cultural and gender studies. Biographical research includes autobiographies, biographies, diaries, oral histories, family stories, and letters. Because these different types of documents can be written for a variety of purposes and audiences, special evaluation techniques need to be brought into play when using biographical writings.

Biographical research can involve:

- studying the life and social context of a famous person who had a significant impact on society, such as Susan B. Anthony;
- developing an enhanced understanding of the works of a particular author, such as Virginia Woolf;
- researching the lives of lesser-known individuals—such as slaves setting up the Underground Railroad—to develop a sense of how people experienced a particular historical event or time period.

DEVELOP A STRATEGY

Decide what types of resources you are looking for and how much information you need. Biographical resources can be scholarly, like a critical biography of a famous political figure that is based on extensive papers, letters, and interviews; or popular, like the autobiography of a movie star written in a casual "tell-all" style. Biographical resources can also be primary (written by the subject) or secondary (writing based on analysis of primary resources, including diary entries and letters).

- If you need brief information, use an online biographical reference source available from your library web page. Many of these sources are listed below. Biographical reference works can range from a few sentences to several pages of analysis.
- If you need extensive information, look for a book-length published autobiography or biography using the techniques described below.
- If the person you are researching is not famous enough to have warranted a published biography, look for an unpublished autobiography, an oral history, letters, or possibly a diary.
- Use free biographical web sites with caution. Rely first on scholarly web databases subscribed to by your library. Biographical information provided on the free web is not always reliable—there are some wonderful, reputable sites which are mentioned below, but there are also many web sites that have not been reviewed, fact-checked, or edited for accuracy.

FIND CRITICAL ESSAYS AND BRIEF FACTUAL INFORMATION

Reference resources, both online and in print, provide factual information and critical essays written by scholars about the life and work of an individual. These tools vary enormously in scope, from large, full-text databases covering hundreds of thousands of people to small, one-volume encyclopedias devoted to a specific category of individuals (such as modern French writers or African American social leaders).

The most effective research strategy is to begin with some of the large online compilations that may be subscribed to by your library. The titles listed below can be found in your library online catalog by doing a title search or by checking your library's web site under "Electronic Resources" or "Databases." Many of these tools have a print counterpart if the online tool is not available at your library.

If the individual you are studying is not contained in these large collections, the next step is to use an online index that will point you to the resources that contain information on your subject. An additional step, often worth making, is to look for specialized directories, dictionaries, or encyclopedias that cover a particular ethnic group, occupation group, geographic location, or other category that sets your person apart from others. Information on how to locate these specialized sources is also listed below.

Use a Full-Text Database for Critical Essays and Factual Information

Most of the large databases listed in this section have search capabilities that allow you to locate individuals by a variety of specifications: occupation, ethnicity or country of origin, date of birth or death, titles of works published, and other categories, including name searches. Many of these sources have broad inclusion criteria so that individuals who had some impact on society during their lifetime (though they may not be famous) are included.

American National Biography (ANB)
This major undertaking carried out by over 6,000 authors and countless editors contains 17,500 biographies in the print version and over 18,000 online. Viewed as the successor to the *Dictionary of American Biography* written in the early 1900s, the *ANB* has broadened the original criteria for inclusion. The *ANB* includes entries about deceased men and women from all time periods and walks of life whose lives have contributed in some significant way to the United States. This encyclopedia provides critical essays with bibliographies of key articles and books on each individual. This resource is available in print and online in many libraries.

Biography Reference Bank (includes *Wilson Biographies Plus* and *Biography Index Plus*)
This source contains indexes and full text for almost 100,000 biographies and obituaries from more than 100 biographical reference books and journals, including the reference title *Current Biography*. Biographical subjects that have been indexed range from antiquity to the present and represent all fields and nationalities. This resource is available online in many libraries.

Biography Resource Center and *Who's Who* series
This database contains over 400,000 biographies culled from many different print and online sources, full-text articles from hundreds of journals, magazines, and reference books, as well as access to an additional one million articles from the *Complete Marquis Who's Who*. This resource is available online in many libraries.

Oxford Dictionary of National Biography
This resource is a collection of fifty thousand specially written biographies of men and women who are no longer living who have shaped all aspects of the British past, from the earliest known history through 2000. The articles provide critical analysis as well as citations to key articles and books on each subject. This resource is available in print and online in many libraries.

Additional *Who's Who* and *Who Was Who* books can be found using the online library catalog and combining the keyword search *"Who's Who"* with the criteria you are looking for (e.g., theater, African Americans, nursing, international banking, etc.). For a complete list of these titles, see *Index to Marquis' Who's Who Publications*.

Encyclopedia Britannica

Encyclopedia Britannica includes more than seventy thousand encyclopedia articles and year-in-review articles from recent yearbooks. The database provides a search engine to find articles containing biographical information. This resource is available in print and online in many libraries.

Literature Resource Center

This database includes full-text biographical entries, factual information, and critical analysis on authors from all time periods and countries. Entries are written by scholars. Some entries include photographs or sketches. This source is available online in many libraries and is also available in print under the titles *Contemporary Authors* and *Dictionary of Literary Biography*.

In addition to the collections mentioned above, there are many print encyclopedias that can be consulted if your library does not subscribe to the online collections or if the person you seek is not listed in the above sources. The following titles are useful biographical encyclopedias:

- *Almanac of Famous People*
- *American Men and Women of Science*
- *Cambridge Biographical Encyclopedia*
- *Cambridge Dictionary of American Biography*
- *Chambers Biographical Dictionary*
- *Current Biography*
- *Dictionary of American Negro Biography*
- *McGraw-Hill Encyclopedia of World Biography*
- *National Cyclopedia of American Biography*
- *Notable American Women, 1607–1950: A Biographical Dictionary*
- *Notable American Women, the Modern Period: A Biographical Dictionary*
- *Webster's New Biographical Dictionary*

Use Specialized Directories, Dictionaries, and Encyclopedias

There are biographical directories, dictionaries, and encyclopedias on every topic imaginable, including *Women Serial and Mass Murderers; American Song Lyricists, 1920–1960*; and *Dictionary of Artists' Models*. Most of these titles are still in print. If the person you are looking for fits into a category of some sort—filmmaker, French writer, Asian American, feminist—then there may be a biographical directory, dictionary, or encyclopedia that will provide information on that person. A directory usually provides brief factual information such as birth and death dates, an address, or an occupation. A dictionary provides more extensive factual information, and an encyclopedia often includes a critical essay and list of key references to pursue.

To find these specialized reference tools that include biographical information, combine a category—occupation, home country, gender, ethnicity, time period—with the words "biography or biographical." For example:

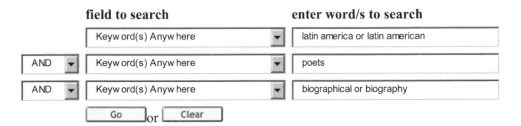

Sometimes adding the following keywords to the search above can narrow the search and will help you to avoid getting individual biographies:

"Encyclopedia or Encyclopedias or Dictionary or Dictionaries"
or
"Encyclopedia* or Dictionar*" (to get singular and plural endings)

One massive index used by many researchers to locate biographical information in large biographical dictionaries, encyclopedias, and books is the *Biography and Genealogy Master Index*. It covers over twelve million historical and contemporary individuals from North America and Western Europe. This resource is available in print or online in many libraries.

FIND PUBLISHED AUTOBIOGRAPHIES AND BIOGRAPHIES

Full-length autobiographies and biographies, usually in the form of published books, are invaluable for uncovering detailed comprehensive information about a person's life. The following sections define autobiographies and biographies and provide techniques for locating these works using the online catalog, reference books, and databases. Different search strategies are employed for locating famous people versus lesser-known individuals. Specific techniques for evaluating autobiographies and biographies are also described below.

An *autobiography* is "a self-produced, non-fiction text that tells the story of its writer's life" (Gunzenhauser 2001). Autobiographies are typically written *in retrospect,* toward the end of a person's life, as a review of the internal thoughts intertwined with the public life of the author. The writer of an autobiography constructs the text with the audience in mind, and the writing often resembles a novel with main characters, a hero, and a story of a personal journey of some sort. Re-created dialogue and dramatic scenes are often included. The writer is attempting to convey something to the reader, offering a personal story in order to instruct or teach a lesson, or to develop support for a cause. An autobiography gives the researcher a rare opportunity to learn about the direct experience of an individual (Golby 1994). In many cases autobiographies are formally published by a publisher, in other cases they have been self-published, printed, or compiled long after they were written.

A *biography* is the history of the life of an individual. Often studied by historians, biography is considered nonfiction but has elements of fiction, including a narrative form with clear parameters—the lifetime of a particular individual. Biographies are sometimes written after the subject of the work has died, so the subject is unable to respond to what was written. Biographies differ from autobiographies in that the author of the biography is separate from the person being written about. They are usually written about well-known people or people who have made a significant contribution to society. Biographers usually rely on primary sources—letters, diaries, photographs, and other material produced by the subject or those who knew the subject. Biographers also might interview family and friends of the subject and use secondary materials such as books and journal and newspaper articles.

Biographies are often formally published, but they differ greatly in their objectivity and accuracy. Often more than one biography is written about a famous individual. Biographies can be authorized—meaning the biographer is given access to materials on the subject—but sometimes certain restrictions are placed on an authorized biographer in terms of what can be written. Unauthorized biographers sometimes lack access to important source material, but the biographer is unrestricted in his or her ability to report on the subject. A biography will provide later researchers with footnotes and references that will identify source material on the person being studied.

"Auto/biography" is a term used to indicate that in some cases the line is blurred between autobiographical and biographical writing. Smith and Watson (2001) give several examples of this in their book *Reading Autobiography: A Guide for Interpreting Life Narratives.* One example is a biography by John Edgar Wideman titled *Brothers and Keepers,* in which the author's biography of his brother is interconnected with his own memories and descriptions of their childhood.

Search the Library Online Catalog to Locate an Autobiography or Biography

Autobiographies and biographies can be located by searching a library online catalog by *subject*. A subject search will retrieve any books written about a person. Use the pull-down box to select "Subject" in the online catalog and then type the last name of the person followed by the first name:

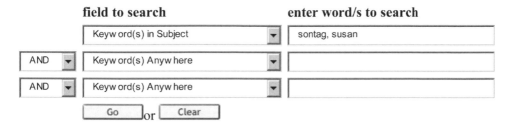

Make sure the name is spelled correctly and that the name is the person's real name and not a pseudonym or stage name.[1] Locate an autobiography by scanning the list by author.

Search Larger Online Catalogs to Locate an Autobiography or Biography

If searching your library online catalog fails to turn up an autobiography or biography by or about your subject, the next step is to try one of the comprehensive library catalogs, *WorldCat* or *RedLightGreen*. These two catalogs represent almost all the books currently held in libraries in the United States, as well as books located in some libraries outside of the United States. *WorldCat* is subscribed to by many libraries, *RedLightGreen* is available for free on the web (a subscription version is titled *Eureka*). These two databases are usually listed alphabetically under "Databases" or "Electronic resources" on the library home page.

Do a subject search in *WorldCat, RedLightGreen*, or *Eureka* similar to the one you did in your home library's online catalog. If you find a book, you can place an interlibrary loan request from your library's web page asking your library to borrow this book.

FIND BIOGRAPHICAL WRITINGS BY LESSER-KNOWN INDIVIDUALS

Researchers frequently study historical events and time periods through the eyes of ordinary individuals with firsthand experience. Biographical databases (listed above) allow category searching by race or ethnicity, gender, birth and death dates, and other categories. These databases indicate where to locate published autobiographies and biographies. In addition, the online catalog can be searched by the characteristics of the group under study.

Search the Library Online Catalog for Lesser-Known Individuals

Many autobiographical accounts are written by individuals who are not famous but who published accounts of their engagement in historical events. In order to find these individuals, search the library online catalog using keywords to describe both the event and the type of writings.

For example, to search for the autobiography of a Native American, the following search could be used:

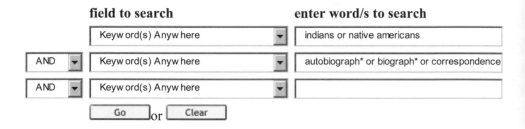

The symbol "*" represents a truncation of the word, instructing the catalog to search for all words that have this root in order to pick up plurals or other endings. Additional keywords could be added to the second box such as "sources" or "personal narratives."

To search for autobiographies or biographies written by veterans of the Persian Gulf War, the following search could be used:

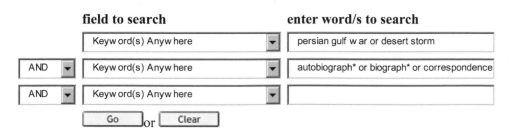

Again, additional keywords such as "sources" or "personal narratives" could be added to the second box.

If a search returns too many "hits" or entries, change from doing a "keyword" search to a "subject heading" search. A subject heading search must use Library of Congress Subject Headings to return results. First, scan the entries your keyword search returned and locate a few books that reflect your needs. Look at the full or detailed record for these books and determine what subject headings were assigned. Once you have the proper subject heading for your topic (e.g., "Indians of North America" or "legislators" or "biologists"), then return to the search screen and combine your subject heading with the subject headings used to indicate biographical writings. For example:

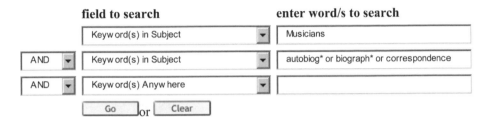

Again, subject headings such as "sources" or "personal narratives" could be added to the second box in this search.

For an even more precise search, you can attach the word "biography" to a Library of Congress Subject Heading and find biographies and autobiographies using the "subject" search. Some common subject headings are:

"Authors French Biography" (or "Authors Latin American," etc.)
"Women Biography"
"African Americans Biography"
"Chemists Biography" (or "Biologists" or "Physicians," etc.)
"Prime Ministers Great Britain Biography" (or "Presidents United States Biography")

If you do not find enough materials at your home institution you can search the larger compilations of library catalogs at either *WorldCat* or *RedLight Green*. Then use the interlibrary loan form on your library web page to request that your library borrow the materials from another institution.

Search the Online Library Catalog for Anthologies or Bibliographies

Reflecting current academic trends, numerous anthologies (collections of writings) and bibliographies (descriptive lists of titles) for autobiographical writings by lesser-known individuals have recently been published. These resources are often used to find autobiographical writings by certain types of people who have been historically underrepresented. For example, to locate biographical material about a type of individual, such as a gypsy, search the online catalog:

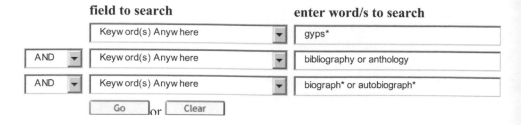

The symbol "*" represents a truncation of the word, instructing the catalog to search for all words that have this root in order to pick up plurals or other endings. The search retrieves anthologies or bibliographies of writings by gypsies such as *Gypsies: A Multidisciplinary Annotated Bibliography.*

An anthology of autobiographies is a collection of autobiographies that is contained in one or several volumes. Anthologies usually focus on a specific group or type of people. The following is a selective list of examples of recent anthologies.

African American Slave Narratives: An Anthology

America in an Arab Mirror: Images of America in Arabic Travel Literature: An Anthology, 1895–1995

American Lives: An Anthology of Autobiographical Writing

Bearing Witness: Selections from African-American Autobiography in the Twentieth Century

The British Migrant Experience, 1700–2000: An Anthology

Native American Autobiography: An Anthology

Nurses at the Front: Writing the Wounds of the Great War

Passages: An Anthology of the Southeast Asian Refugee Experience

Personal Disclosures: An Anthology of Self-Writings from the Seventeenth Century

Pillars of Salt: An Anthology of Early American Criminal Narratives

Wall Tappings: An International Anthology of Women's Prison Writings, 200 to the present

War Wives: A Second World War Anthology

A bibliography of autobiographies is a descriptive list of autobiographical writings by a certain category of individuals. It usually provides several access points such as occupation or time period. Unlike anthologies, bibliographies do not provide the text of the autobiographies, but provide the information necessary to track down the autobiographies. The following is a selective list of bibliographies.

An Annotated Bibliography of American Indian and Eskimo Autobiographies

Autobiographies by Americans of Color 1980–1994: An Annotated Bibliography

Autobiographies by Americans of Color, 1995–2000: An Annotated Bibliography
A Bibliography of American Autobiographies (this corresponds to a collection
   of full-text autobiographies in microfilm)
Black Americans in Autobiography; An Annotated Bibliography of Autobi-
   ographies and Autobiographical Books Written since the Civil War
First Person Female American: A Selected and Annotated Bibliography of the
   Autobiographies of American Women Living after 1950
Musicians' Autobiographies: An Annotated Bibliography of Writings
   Available in English, 1800 to 1980
Scientists since 1660: A Bibliography of Biographies
A Select Bibliography of South African Autobiographies
Through a Woman's I: An Annotated Bibliography of American Women's Au-
   tobiographical Writings, 1946–1976

CRITICALLY EVALUATE AUTOBIOGRAPHIES AND BIOGRAPHIES

Historians use biographical writing to piece together how individuals lived at a particular point in time and how key players fit into the events of the time. Writings from hundreds of years ago focused on recording chronological events, while later biographical writings became more philosophical and recorded analyses in addition to facts. In the past century autobiographies and biographies have become more psychological and self-reflective. They have also become more like novels—stories with a beginning, middle, and end. Sometimes conversation is re-created or imagined, and the line between nonfiction and fiction has become blurred.

Despite all these changes, biographical writings have continued to be viewed as "truthful" and are read as nonfiction accounts. Though no autobiography or biography is completely objective, to a greater or lesser degree they record the thoughts and ideas of a particular individual—the subject themselves or the biographer—at a particular moment in time. Biographies range on a continuum from objective and scholarly to more interpretive and quasi-fictional. In a scholarly biography there will be clear evidence of fact collection with a list of persons interviewed and papers and diaries cited. A less thorough biography might make little reference to resources consulted.

Autobiographies depend on the skills of their authors/subjects, though even if their skills are limited, their autobiographies can contain valuable historical material. The researcher must often rely on intuitive reaction when researching autobiographies—does the writer seem sincere, does the writer have an axe to grind, is there an agenda or publicity angle? Though it is impossible to determine the objectivity of a particular work, there are evaluative techniques that can be employed to help the researcher weigh the evidence and determine if the account has enough merit to warrant inclusion in the research being conducted.

Critical Reviews

Find critical reviews of the work. Most reviews are written around the time the work was published. Reviewers will often discuss the perceived accuracy of a book. (Finding book reviews is explained in chapter 2.)

Authenticity

Determine if the work is authentic. Is the work in question really written by the subject, or was there a collaborator or ghost writer? Did the collaborator play a primary or secondary role? Could this work be a forgery? Looking for scholarly articles that have also used the work you are viewing may shed light on any problems inherent in the writing. Check several key dates and places against another reliable source.

Authority/Objectivity

Determine if the work is authoritative. Compare it to other sources that report on the person's life. In reviewing a biography, check the list of references to see if it is extensive and to examine what types of resources were used. Did the biographer rely on both primary and secondary sources? Is there any historical evidence reproduced such as photographs or diary entries? Does the narrative seem fair and objective or was there a particular slant evident? In reviewing an autobiography, think about how it was written. Does it seem honest and sincere? Does it seem comprehensive, or are certain issues and time periods left out? Does it seem to accurately represent what that person was thinking and how he or she viewed his or her life based on other information sources? Is the tone of the book defensive, modest, self-critical, forthright, humorous, self-aggrandizing? How old was the author when he or she wrote the book?

Expertise of Biographer

In the case of biography, determine the credentials and background of the author. Is the author affiliated with an educational institution? Is the author historian, a fan, a literary scholar, or a journalist? Is the author writing on a current subject or looking back through history? If the author had authorization or was even hired to write the biography, he or she may have had access to more resources, but also may have made an agreement to refrain from mentioning certain issues. If the author was unauthorized, he or she may have been refused permission to view certain personal papers or denied interviews with relevant individuals. What type of review process was in place for the work? If it was published by a scholarly or academic press or journal, then peer review (other experts evaluating the work before it is published) can ensure a more reliable product.

Comparison to Other Accounts

Weigh the report against other accounts that have been written about the event, time period, or individual.

Motivation of Author

Ask yourself why the author wrote the book. Who was the author's perceived audience and what was the author trying to convey? What motivated the author? In the case of autobiography, was it a wish for immortality, a desire to set the record straight, or an attempt to justify a particular action? What did it mean to be an author at that time in history? Who would benefit from a particular work being published? How was the work received when it originally came out? Who would have read the work at the time? In the case of biography, is the author a fan or an enemy of the subject, or does the author seem objective? Biographers are not always impartial toward their subjects.

Researcher Bias

Keep in mind your own baggage. What do you bring to the reading of the work? Remember that you are interpreting the biographical writings based on your own life experiences, belief systems, and biases.

FIND DIARIES

Diary writing differs from autobiography in that it does not look back over a period of life and reconstruct it; it is instead an ongoing account of events and feelings as viewed through the eyes of one individual, and is contemporaneous with the life of that individual.

Diaries vary widely in scope and style, ranging from daily lists of the writer's activities to sporadic philosophical or intimate reflections about the writer's family, friends, and work. Diaries are kept for a variety of reasons—sometimes they are an attempt to understand a life, to remember particular events and people, or to record history as it is experienced. Though diary writing is often seen as private and personal, the act of writing has a public aspect to it. There is sometimes an awareness by the writer that the entries might one day be made public.

Diaries or journals can frequently provide more personal views and authentic reactions to events because the writer is unencumbered by the processes imposed on him or her by the publishing process. Diaries help the researcher understand an individual's experience in a more nuanced way and provide internal information that is not available through a published source.

Use the Online Library Catalog to Find Diaries

Diaries can be found in the library online catalog by using a keyword search combining the word "diaries" with a person's name, a category or group of people, or historical event. Sometimes the word "personal narratives" is used instead of the word "diaries." The following examples illustrate ways to search the catalog:

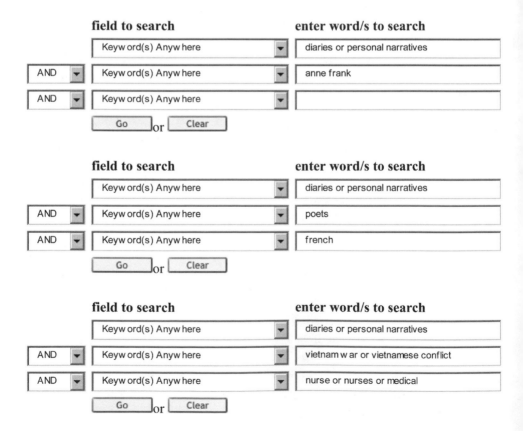

Always use synonyms for keywords that could be cataloged more than one way. Nurses could be singular or plural or even be referred to as medical personnel or medical staff. Similarly, the Vietnam War could also be referred to as the Vietnamese Conflict, which is the official Library of Congress Subject Heading.

The above searches could also be done as "subject" searches if you know the proper Library of Congress Subject Heading. The subject heading can be found by doing a keyword search first and finding the heading in the record of a relevant book. It can also be found by checking the Library of Congress web site at http://authorities.loc.gov/. The following are examples of valid subject headings:

"Isherwood, Christopher, Diaries"
"French Diaries"
"Authors, French, Diaries"
"Nurses, Personal Narratives"
"Military Nursing, Personal Narratives"
"Vietnamese Conflict, 1961–1975, Personal Narratives"

Search Larger Online Catalogs to Locate Diaries

If searching your library online catalog fails to turn up a diary, the next step is to go to a much larger library catalog: *WorldCat* or *RedLightGreen*. These two catalogs represent almost all of the books currently held in libraries in the United States, as well as books located in some libraries outside of the United States. Many academic libraries subscribe to *WorldCat*, and *RedLightGreen* is available for free on the web. *WorldCat* is usually listed under "databases" or "electronic resources" on the library home page. Do a keyword search in either *WorldCat* or *RedLightGreen* similar to the one you did in your home library's online catalog.

Search Online Collections of Diaries

Though most diaries remain in print form—either published or housed in archives—some diaries have been digitized and are available in full text online. The following is a selective list of collections of diaries available online. Most are free, but some are only available through library subscriptions. Additional databases containing full text or indexing to diaries and other primary source material can be found in chapter 4.

The African American Odyssey: A Quest for Full Citizenship (Library of Congress, *American Memory Project*)

http://memory.loc.gov/ammem/aaohtml/exhibit/aointro.html
This site includes twenty letters and diaries relating to African American history from the early national period through the twentieth century.

American Civil War: Letters and Diaries (Alexander Street Press)
This collection is drawn from both published and unpublished letters, diaries, and memoirs. The database provides searches by many different criteria, including race, gender, occupation, military rank, educational level, and others. (Library subscription required.)

American Memory: Historical Collections for the National Digital Library (Library of Congress)
http://lcweb2.loc.gov/ammem/amhome.html
This collection provides full text of many diaries and personal narratives relating to American history.

Civil War Women (Duke University)
http://scriptorium.lib.duke.edu/women/cwdocs.html
This is a collection of diaries, letters, and other primary sources written by women during the Civil War in the United States.

First-Person Narratives of the American South (University of North Carolina)
http://docsouth.unc.edu/fpn/fpn.html
This collection contains diaries and letters relating to the culture of the American south in the late nineteenth and early twentieth centuries. The collection includes the narratives and first-person accounts of women, African Americans, laborers, and Native Americans.

North American Women's Letters and Diaries, Colonial to 1950 (Alexander Street Press)
The collection includes over 100,000 pages of published letters and diaries from Colonial times to 1950, and 7,000 pages of previously unpublished materials. The letters and diaries are drawn from several hundred sources, including journal articles, pamphlets, newsletters, books, and conference proceedings. The records represent every age group, many ethnic groups, geographical regions, and famous and lesser-known individuals. (Library subscription required.)

Valley of the Shadow (University of Virginia)
http://jefferson.village.virginia.edu/vshadow2
This archive includes over five hundred letters and diaries relating to two communities—Staunton, Virginia, and Chambersburg, Pennsylvania—before, during, and after the Civil War.

Find Anthologies and Bibliographies of Diaries

There are a limited number of anthologies (collections) and bibliographies (annotated lists of titles) of diaries. The following lists include titles that are available at most research libraries. The anthologies contain the text of diaries either within the bound volume or in a companion microfilm set that goes with the print. The bibliographies are useful for tracking down diaries. Historically, diary-keeping was more prevalent among women. The lists below reflect that fact.

Anthologies

Capacious Hold-All: An Anthology of Englishwomen's Diary Writings
Covered Wagon Women: Diaries and Letters from the Western Trail, 1840–1890
A Day at a Time: The Diary Literature of American Women from 1764 to the Present
Diaries of Girls and Women: A Midwestern American Sampler
Diaries of Ireland: An Anthology, 1590–1987
English Family Life, 1576–1716: An Anthology from Diaries
Ho for California!: Women's Overland Diaries from the Huntington Library
Private Pages: Diaries of American Women, 1830s–1970s
A Treasury of the World's Great Diaries
Women's Diaries of the Westward Journey

Anthologies with Companion Microfilm Collections

American Women's Diaries: New England Women
American Women's Diaries: Southern Women
American Women's Diaries: Western Women
British Manuscript Diaries of the Nineteenth Century: An Annotated Listing
New England Women and Their Families in the 18th and 19th Centuries: Personal Papers, Letters and Diaries
Records of Ante-bellum Southern Plantations from the Revolution through the Civil War
Southern Women and Their Families in the Nineteenth Century, Papers and Diaries
Travels in the Confederate States
Travels in the New South
Travels in the Old South

Bibliographies

American Diaries: An Annotated Bibliography of Published American Diaries and Journals

American Diaries in Manuscript, 1580–1954: A Descriptive Bibliography

American Diaries of World War II

And So to Bed: A Bibliography of Diaries Published in English

British Women's Diaries: A Descriptive Bibliography of Selected Nineteenth-Century Women's Manuscript Diaries

Civil War Eyewitnesses: An Annotated Bibliography of Books and Articles, 1955–1986

Personal Accounts of Events, Travels, and Everyday Life in America: An Annotated Bibliography

Personal Writings by Women to 1900: A Bibliography of American and British Writers

The Published Diaries and Letters of American Women: An Annotated Bibliography

Travels in the Confederate States: A Bibliography

Women's Diaries, Journals, and Letters: An Annotated Bibliography

Women's Language and Experience, 1500–1940: Women's Diaries and Related Sources

CRITICALLY EVALUATE DIARIES

Diaries can be fascinating to read and they provide a better cross-sectional view of the historical record than other sources. Though they are limited to those who were literate, and were more often kept by women than men, they reflect a diverse range of people from a variety of backgrounds, including middle-class and wealthy, old and young, men and women. Historians and women's studies scholars frequently use diaries to pull together information about women's experiences, which were typically underrepresented in more official publications such as newspapers or government documents.

Although diaries are private documents, they reflect the shared conventions of the particular time period during which they were produced. Both the style of writing and the content are greatly influenced by time period. Historians often study groups of diaries to find the commonalities stemming from a particular period in history. During the seventeenth century diaries were used as a way for an individual to chart his or her spiritual progress (Stowe 2004). Later diaries were used to explore and record feelings, personal reflections, and intellectual ideas. By the early 1800s diarists started to use literary conventions borrowed from novel writing and experimented with styles of creative writing (Stowe 2004). Certain trends in diary writing—such as giving the diary a name, beginning each entry with "Dear Diary," recording the weather, or logging daily activities—occurred at different times in history. Today, web diaries add complexity to the study of personal experiences because the "private" writings of an individual are posted in public spaces on the internet, in a blog, or on a home page.

When conducting any type of biographical research, it is essential to rely on more than one source for any piece of questionable information. Any biographical narrative is inherently flawed. Discovering the flaws, taking them into account, and using the context of the times as well as other primary and secondary sources for verification are essential. Biographical research is exciting, but like detective work it requires a healthy skepticism and the energy to dig deep, as the following example illustrates.

When Virginia Bernhard, a history professor, noticed that a number of scholarly articles referred to Cotton Mather's third wife Lydia as being insane, she decided to investigate further. Cotton Mather, a famous seventeenth century Puritan minister, had kept extensive diaries that have been studied by many historians. Bernhard discovered that each article that mentioned Lydia's insanity could be traced back to a single source—Mather's diary entries.

On further investigation Dr. Bernhard found numerous pieces of evidence that called into question Cotton Mather's appraisal of his wife.

—Mather had a tendency to use similar language when describing foes who disagreed with him;

—his mentions of Lydia's mental instability came during a time of extreme family stress but these descriptions stopped when the household became more settled;

—this wife was more independent and strong-willed than his previous wives and did not act "properly" for a woman from that time period.

Though many historians before Bernhard had taken Cotton Mather's appraisal of his wife at face value, Dr. Bernhard was able to convincingly prove, based on the circumstances of the household and the inclusion of other primary documents such as Lydia's obituary and descriptions of her at public events, that Lydia might have been a strong character, but was unlikely to have been insane. (Bernhard 1987)

Some of the following issues should be explored when critically evaluating a diary.

Authenticity and Authorship

It is not always clear who wrote a diary. In addition, some diaries are edited or censored for a variety of reasons. An editor compiling a diary in an anthology might remove pieces of text that are deemed less interesting, or a relative might remove parts of a diary to avoid sharing embarrassing family events. Try to determine if what you are viewing is a complete diary, and think about who might have saved the diary and why.

Mary Chestnut's "diary," relied on extensively by Civil War historians because it was so well written and remarkably prescient, was later found to be compiled more than a decade after the war ended based on notes she had taken during the war (Woodward 1981). Still useful, it was no longer viewed as a diary and the content needed to be interpreted in this new light.

External Consistency

Corroborate particular facts mentioned in the diary. If the writer records going to an important event or watching a public official give a speech, check local newspaper articles to see if that event occurred when the diarist recorded it. This fact-checking serves two purposes: it widens your understanding of the historical time period and checks the accuracy of your diarist. Sometimes it helps to draw a chart to indicate relationships between the diarist and family members, friends, and historical events. It may be necessary to use other sources to determine who is being referred to when the writer says "my uncle" or "my friend John."

Internal Consistency

Read the diary for internal consistency. Is the diarist consistent about issues that are reported? If not, why might there be variation in the reporting? Are there reasons why the diarist might not be completely honest?

Sincerity

Though sincerity is a subjective characteristic to measure, take note of how the diarist reports views and feelings. What is the author's motivation for writing—to internally explore events and feelings for personal self-reflection or to leave some historical record? What was the inspiration for writing the diary? Was it because social conventions called for men or women of a certain social standing to keep a diary, or was there some incident or personal crisis that prompted the writing? A diarist often has some notion that a later audience will be reading his or her work. Does the writing convey that awareness? Might it influence how and what is being reported?

Physicality

The evaluation of diaries should, if possible, involve an analysis of their physical nature. Is the handwriting careful and neat, or hurried and messy?

Is the diary written on scrap paper, suggesting the writer had limited means, or on thick expensive stationery, suggesting wealth and privilege (Woodward 1981)?

Omissions

Observe what the diarist chose to omit from his or her record about an event or person, as well as what he or she chose to include. Were significant facts or important issues left out of the author's writings? Or did the writer only come into contact with a certain segment of the population and report the views of that particular group?

Researcher Bias

Be aware of how the set of values you have might differ from the diarist's value system. You are not neutral. Try not to interpret the diarist's writing in light of your own values, but with knowledge about his or her value system and the ideals of the time period in which he or she wrote. Come up with multiple interpretations of the diary and explore the cultural and psychological undertones of the writing. Always check secondary literature, journal articles, and books to see what previous researchers concluded about a particular issue concerning the diarist or events he or she recorded.

FIND ORAL HISTORIES

Oral history can be defined as "a tape-recorded conversation in which two participants engage in deep discussion about the past. . . . Oral historians engage in collecting and interpreting information about the past through the study of individual experiences relayed in a story form" (Clark 2001). Today, videotaping and other technologies can be added to the process so that a visual image is also preserved.

Oral history is similar to autobiography because it involves a person speaking about his or her life experience. It is also similar to biography because a second person, the interviewer, plays an influential role in the way the story is told. The field of oral history was formally established in the United States in the 1930s when researchers at the Columbia University Oral History Research Office began to record, transcribe, and archive interviews. However, traditional oral histories passed down from one person to another date back to ancient times.

Modern oral history has contributed greatly to the democratization of the historical record by recording the experiences of "ordinary" people who represent diverse backgrounds. These rich narratives provide information about daily life that is not included in the official historical record. Oral histories often provide exciting stories that bring new meaning to historical events and time periods. They are typically converted into written transcripts of the recordings and are available on the web and in microform collections, or are collected in books or library special collections. Sometimes the recordings themselves are also available.

Oral histories have been collected for many different purposes. Some collections focus on particular experiences such as that of Asian American immigrants, or particular historical events such as the Holocaust. Other collections focus on experiences of workers in particular industries or occupations, such as factory workers or engineers. Sometimes researchers carry out quantitative analyses on these interviews by compiling accounts from a particular population group and then teasing out common experiences or similar reactions to events. Oral history is used in many disciplines in addition to history such as anthropology, education, ethnic studies, literature, sociology, women's studies, and gerontology.

Search Oral History Web Sites

The study of oral history is growing because of scholars' increasing interest in studying the lives and experiences of "ordinary" people. Oral histories have also become a more accepted tool for research when used in combination with other resources. The internet provides access to many rich oral history collections, some of which allow the researcher to listen to an audio recording as well as read a transcript. Hearing the words spoken can provide additional contextual information and access to the feelings and inflection used by the narrator when speaking.

The selective list below includes only those web sites that contain either transcripts or recordings online. For extensive lists of oral history collections, see the University of Connecticut Center for Oral History (www.ucc.uconn.edu/~cohadm01/links.html). For large collections of oral histories from university sites, see the Louisiana State University T. Harry Williams Center for Oral History (http://www.lib.lsu.edu/special/williams/links.html).

American Memory Project (Library of Congress)
http://memory.loc.gov/ammem/
This site includes several large oral history collections, including manuscripts from the Federal Writers' Project.

American Slave Narratives: An Online Anthology (University of Virginia)
http://xroads.virginia.edu/~hyper/wpa/wpahome.html

This site includes interviews done by the Works Progress Administration with thousands of former slaves between 1936 and 1938. Slave narratives can also be found in the print source *The American Slave: A Composite Autobiography*.

Archives of American Art (Smithsonian)
http://www.archivesofamericanart.si.edu/oralhist/oralhist.htm
This site includes over three thousand interviews done for AAA's oral history program. Selected transcripts are available online.

Civil Rights Digital Archive (University of Southern Mississippi)
http://www.lib.usm.edu/~spcol/crda
This site contains oral history resources on the Civil Rights movement.

IEEE History Center (Institute of Electrical and Electronics Engineers)
http://www.ieee.org/organizations/history_center/oral_histories.html
This collection includes hundreds of oral histories with technologists from the twentieth century.

Oral History Online (Alexander Street Press)
The largest index of English-language oral histories, this database provides keyword searching of transcripts and links to full text. Released in 2004, this resource is eventually expected to cover 300,000 interviews from more than 2,300 collections. (Library subscription required.)

Rutgers Oral History Archives (Rutgers University)
http://fas-history.rutgers.edu/oralhistory/home.html
This site includes transcripts of interviews from men and women who served abroad and on the home front during World War II, the Korean War, the Vietnam War, and the Cold War.

Social Security Administration Oral Histories (Social Security Administration)
http://www.ssa.gov/history/orallist.html
This site contains transcripts of oral histories from key players involved in the history of the Social Security Administration as well as excerpts from other collections, including presidential libraries and the Oral History Center at Columbia University.

University of California at Berkeley Regional Oral History Office (The Bancroft Library, UC Berkeley)
http://bancroft.berkeley.edu/ROHO/
This is one of the best oral history sites for online access. It contains a wide variety of collections, including oral histories on Earl Warren, criminal justice, suffragists, disability rights, the arts, and legal history.

Women in Journalism Oral History Project (Washington Press Club Foundation)
http://npc.press.org/wpforal.ohhome.htm
This site includes about sixty interviews with women journalists who have made significant contributions to society since the 1920s through careers in journalism.

Search the Online Catalog to Find Oral Histories

There are several ways to search your library online catalog for oral history transcripts that have been collected in books or other formats. One strategy is to search using the keyword:

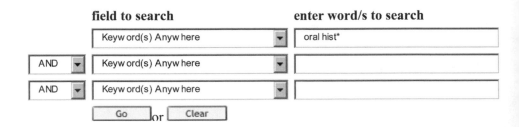

The "*" retrieves both "oral history" and "oral histories." Scan through the list of titles and choose one that interests you.

If you are looking for a specific type of oral history, combine the subject you are looking for with the terms "oral history" or "interview." For example:

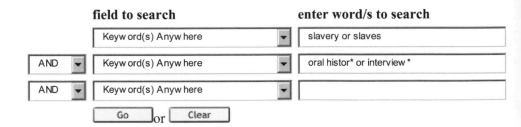

The "*" retrieves the plural or a word with another ending that shares the same root.

Many libraries own large collections of oral histories on microfilm. An example is the famous *Columbia University Oral History Project*. These collections can be found by using the searches listed above. The following is a selective list of some of the larger collections that are held by many libraries.

The American Indian Oral History Collection

Asian American Experiences in the United States: Oral Histories of First to Fourth Generation Americans from China, the Philippines, Japan, India, the Pacific Islands, Vietnam, and Cambodia

Civil Rights during the Johnson Administration

Columbia University Oral History Project

Italians in Chicago Oral History Project

Listening to Indians

The Twentieth Century Trade Union Woman: Vehicle for Social Change

Voices from Ellis Island: An Oral History of American Immigration

The Worker and Technological Change 1930–1980: Interviews with Connecticut Workers

CRITICALLY EVALUATE ORAL HISTORIES

Oral histories were originally seen as a limited means of studying history due to their lack of objectivity and the unreliability and instability of individual memory. Today they are more widely accepted by scholars as one of many tools historians can use to attempt to reconstruct the past. Oral historians acknowledge both the benefits and shortcomings of having direct personal contact with those being researched (Reinharz and Davidman 1992).

Oral histories can be seductive and persuasive. These interesting firsthand accounts can easily sway even an experienced researcher. Verifying an oral history with other knowledge and resources is vital. An oral history is not the simple reporting of facts but rather "an interpretive event, as the narrator compresses years of living into a few hours of talk, selecting, consciously and unconsciously, what to say and how to say it" (Shopes 2004).

The following issues should be considered when evaluating oral histories.

Understand the Social Lens of the Narrator

What are the social and cultural biases of the narrator? Race, gender, background, and personal experiences all influence how the narrator views his or her world and reports on it. Does the narrator have a particular agenda or a need to present something in an especially favorable or unfavorable light? What was the social climate like at the moment when the interview was conducted and how might this influences the way the narrator interprets and reports on an event? In addition, take into account the limitations of individual memory. No one remembers an event exactly as it occurs, and many factors influence and shape the recounting of an event.

Determine the Mission of the Interviewer

The questions the interviewer chooses to ask greatly influence the content of the oral history. The questions stem from the interviewer's interpretation of what is historically important and what the interviewer feels is the purpose of the oral history (Shopes 2004). The degree of comfort and safety the narrator feels with the interviewer has an impact on what is discussed. The skill and preparation level of the interviewer, his or her social and cultural background, the atmosphere and comfort of the setting in which the interview is conducted, and any prior relationship between the interviewer and the narrator all influence the story told (Shopes 2004).

When oral history was first used as a research tool, historians attempted to be impartial, objective, and passive players in the interview. More recent oral historians recognized the weakness of this approach and acknowledge the active role that the interviewer plays in overtly influencing the process (Roberts 2002).

Check for Internal Consistency

Assess the entire story the narrator relates. Check to see if the narrator is consistent in describing particular events. If there are inconsistencies, explore possible explanations for these inconsistencies. Consider the reliability of the narrator and his or her ability to relate events.

Check for External Consistency

Compare the story told by the narrator to accounts given in other historical documents and secondary articles and books. If the stories differ, try to determine why. Perhaps the agenda or bias of the narrator differs from the motivation of the writer of another document (Shopes 2004).

Determine the Purpose of the Oral History

Is the oral history part of a larger collection of oral histories? Skim the content to figure out if there is a particular focus. Are the questions predominantly related to public events or intimate life experiences? Try to determine the purpose of the collection and how this might influence the structure of the interviews and the content of the reporting. For example, an oral history that is part of a collection relating to the immigrant experience in America might heavily focus on issues such as hardship, poverty, and racism.

VALIDATE BIOGRAPHICAL WRITINGS USING SECONDARY SOURCES

Journal, newspaper, and magazine articles can provide biographical information about famous individuals as well as background information about events and the time period in which an individual lived. They are also useful for externally validating the information gleaned from biographical writings.

Finding scholarly journals, newspapers, and magazines articles is explained in chapter 3, finding historical newspaper and magazine articles is explained in chapter 4. Choosing the right journal database will depend largely on the person you are researching. For example, *Art Abstracts* would be the best journal index to use for research on a particular artist. Journal and magazine articles frequently publish interviews with well-known figures. Sometimes these interviews are the only biographical material available on a particular individual. Articles often focus on a specific aspect of a person's life and can be great for detailed analysis. For less famous people, locating an obituary in a newspaper can provide essential though limited information.

USE BIOGRAPHICAL WEB SITES WITH CAUTION

If you do a Google search on Helen Keller to find out when she was born, when she went blind and deaf, and when she died, you will find hundreds of biographical web sites that provide this information. Unfortunately, the web sites differ in their accounts, providing different dates for each of these events. When searching the web for biographical information, go to a reputable site and then enter the name you are looking for, rather than entering a search in Google. This section contains web sites that:

- provide large collections of authoritative biographies;
- provide extensive links to biographical web sites;
- provide biographical information about a specific population.

Web Sites with Authoritative Biographies

Biographical Dictionary (S 9 Technologies)
http://www.s9.com/biography/
This source includes thousands of brief biographical sketches. It covers more historical than contemporary figures.

Biography.com (A&E Television Networks)
http://www.biography.com

This site provides brief authoritative factual information on thousands of famous people.

Columbia Encyclopedia (Bartleby.com)
http://www.bartleby.com/65/
The online version of *The Columbia Encyclopedia* includes brief biographical sketches of famous people.

PBS—History (Public Broadcasting System)
http://www.pbs.org/history/history_biographies.html
The PBS site includes information from biographical documentaries broadcast on the network.

Web Sites with Links to Collections of Biographical Resources

Biographical Information (LibrarySpot)
http://www.libraryspot.com/biographies/
This site provides links to a large collection of reputable biography web sites.

Biographical Resources (Internet Public Library)
http://www.ipl.org/div/subject/browse/ref15.00.00/
This site provides an extensive list of links to biographical information.

Biographical Web Sites That Have a Specific Focus

Biographical Directory of the United States Congress
http://bioguide.congress.gov/biosearch/biosearch.asp

First Ladies of the United States
http://www.whitehouse.gov/history/firstladies/

4000 Years of Women in Science
http://www.astr.ua.edu/4000WS/summary.shtml

Mathematicians
http://www-groups.dcs.st-and.ac.uk/~history/BiogIndex.html

Nobel Prize Internet Archive
http://www.almaz.com/nobel/

Presidents of the United States
http://ipl.org/ref/POTUS/

The Pulitzer Prizes
http://www.pulitzer.org/

Supreme Court Justices
http://www.oyez.org/oyez/portlet/justices/

CRITICALLY EVALUATE BIOGRAPHICAL WEB SITES

Biographical information found on the web, outside of published biographical databases that are purchased by libraries, can vary widely in its accuracy and validity. The following strategies can be used, in addition to the techniques described throughout this chapter, when it is necessary to cull biographical information from unpublished web sources.

Purpose

Determine the purpose of the site you are viewing. Did educators create it for educational purposes, or are there advertisements or fees charged for viewing information on the site?

Authority

Determine who is responsible for the site. Was it set up by one individual or by an organization? If an organization is responsible, what are the goals of that organization? Is it possible to email someone at the site to ask questions? Where did the biographical information come from? Was it written by one person, by scholars, or by college students?

Objectivity and Accuracy

Try to determine if the information is being presented objectively or if there seems to be a tone or slant to the writing. Did a fan or someone with a personal interest in the subject write the biography? Fact-checkers, proofreaders, and editors are much less commonly associated with the development of web pages. Web pages that were originally published as books might have more accurate content than other types of web pages. Always use other sources to verify information found on web pages.

Currency

How current is the material being presented? Does the date on the page (if there is one) represent when the material was written, when the material was put online, or when the material was revised?

Connections to Other Pages

Try to view each web page separately. Sometimes sites with links to each other vary in their reliability. In other words, there are authoritative biographical directories on the web that link to some questionable sources.

Longevity

Try to determine the stability of the web site. A web site created by an organization such as the Nobel Prize Internet Archive or an educational institution is probably more stable than one created by an unaffiliated individual.

NOTE

1. In some cases an author is listed under his or her pseudonym if the author is better known under that name. For example, Mark Twain is listed under Twain and not his real name, Samuel Clemens.

REFERENCES

Bernhard, Virginia. 1987. Cotton Mather's "most unhappy wife": Reflections on the uses of historical evidence. *New England Quarterly* 60, no. 3 (September): 341–362.

Clark, Mary Marshall. 2001. Oral history. In *Encyclopedia of life writing: Autobiographical and biographical forms*, edited by Margaretta Jolly. London, Chicago: Fitzroy Dearborn. 677–680.

Golby, John. 1994. Autobiographies, letters and diaries. In *Sources and methods for family and community historians: A handbook*, edited by Michael Drake and Ruth Finnegan. Cambridge: Cambridge University Press.

Gunzenhauser, Bonnie J. 2001. Autobiography. In *Encyclopedia of life writing: Autobiographical and biographical forms*, edited by Margaretta Jolly. London, Chicago: Fitzroy Dearborn. 75–78.

Reinharz, Shulamit, with Lynn Davidman. 1992. *Feminist methods in social research*. New York: Oxford University Press.

Roberts, Brian. 2002. *Biographical research*. Buckingham, Philadelphia: Open University Press.

Shopes, Linda. What is oral history. *History Matters: The U.S. Survey on the Web.* http://historymatters.gmu.edu/mse/oral/what.html. Accessed April 30, 2004.

Smith, Sidonie, and Julia Watson. 2001. *Reading autobiography: A guide for interpreting life narratives*. Minneapolis: University of Minnesota Press.

Stowe, Steven. Making sense of letters and diaries. *History Matters: The U.S. Survey on the Web.* http://historymatters.gmu.edu/mse/letters/. Accessed April 2, 2004.

Woodward, C. Vann, ed. 1981. *Mary Chestnut's Civil War*. New Haven, CT: Yale University Press.

6

Legal Research

While some look to the Internet as an innovative vehicle for commu-
nication, the court continues to warily and wearily view it largely as
one large catalyst for rumor, innuendo and misinformation.

Samuel B. Kent, United States District Judge[1]

Judges and lawyers, like the rest of the world, are increasingly relying on the
internet to look up information, check facts, and investigate issues (McDonough 2004). Unfortunately, some resort to Google searches and pull information off web pages rather than searching reputable and scholarly sources
that have been through some type of editorial review and fact-checking.

In the above quotation, Judge Kent reflects the legal community's reser-
vations in using web sites as evidence in court cases. In this case the plaintiff brought claims for personal injuries sustained while working on a boat
owned by Johnny's Oyster & Shrimp. Johnny's denied owning the boat on
which the plaintiff worked, and the plaintiff used a coast guard web site
vessel database to try to prove Johnny's owned the boat in question. The
court dismissed the case, stating that:

> Anyone can put anything on the Internet. No Web-site is monitored for accuracy and
> nothing contained therein is under oath or even subject to independent verification
> absent underlying documentation. Moreover, the Court holds no illusions that hack-
> ers can adulterate the content on any web-site from any location at any time.[2]

The internet has transformed legal research because most court cases,
statutes, law review articles, and other legal resources are now available

online. However, Google searching is not yet the answer for legal researchers. Specialized legal databases and search engines must be employed to ensure that online legal information is legitimate and authoritative.

FIND PRIMARY AND SECONDARY LEGAL RESOURCES

Legal research consists of locating and analyzing both primary and secondary resources. The primary documents in legal research are:

- case law: judicial decisions or "judge-made" law and related resources such as legal briefs and oral arguments;
- statutes: legislative law—bills passed by Congress;
- regulations: rules developed by executive branch agencies to interpret and define broader statutory law.

This chapter will cover U.S. case law and secondary resources. Statutory and regulatory law are covered in chapter 7, "Government Documents and Statistics."

Secondary resources for legal research include:

- newspapers and magazines;
- legal encyclopedias;
- books;
- scholarly law review and law journal articles.

This chapter covers the U.S. court system, strategies for searching legal databases for cases and analysis, finding secondary legal resources, locating specific court cases and types of cases, determining if a case is still "good law," and critically evaluating different types of legal information.

FIND CASE LAW

The United States has two judicial systems that parallel each other. The federal court system includes the Supreme Court, the thirteen courts of appeal, and the ninety-four district courts. In addition, there are several special district courts—such as the U.S. Court of International Trade—that deal with particular types of federal cases. Each state has a system of courts that includes a state supreme court, state appellate courts, state trial courts, and county and municipal courts.

Case law consists of judicial opinions and is sometimes referred to as "judge-made" law to differentiate it from laws passed by the legislature or regulations passed by administrative agencies. Because laws passed by Congress are often broad, court decisions assist in the interpretation of the law by applying it to a specific situation.

All case law is based on the doctrine of *stare decisis*, Latin for "to stand by that which is decided." The U.S. legal system relies on past legal decisions (past *precedent*) to decide current cases. This doctrine is based on a notion of fairness—people in similar situations should be dealt with in a similar manner, and judgments should be consistent so that people can predict the consequences of future actions.

When lawyers conduct research on a case they are looking for prior similar cases, decided by the highest court possible that is located in the same jurisdiction and has not been overruled or modified. If a similar case is found, called a "case in point," its decision will be binding on a lower court deciding on the same type of case. A decision made from the same jurisdiction is considered "mandatory authority" and is binding on a lower court. Decisions from courts in other jurisdictions are considered "persuasive authority" and are considered but not necessarily followed.

Use Effective Techniques for Searching Legal Databases

A great deal of case law is available online. The rule of thumb is the higher the court, the easier it is to get decisions as well as briefs, oral arguments, and related materials. The two best sources for case law are LexisNexis and Westlaw. Both of these commercial databases are available through many academic library web pages. They provide access to case law and include links to related laws, cases, law review articles, and legal encyclopedia articles that analyze points of law.

LexisNexis and Westlaw allow general searches across courts and will customize a search to look for decisions from only one court, such as the Supreme Court. If possible, first narrow your search to a specific court or level of court (such as district courts or a particular state court). If you do not know the court, check secondary sources such as newspaper or journal articles before searching a legal database. There are also free web resources containing case law. FindLaw (www.findlaw.com) is a database containing Supreme Court, appellate court, and district court decisions. Cornell Law School hosts the Legal Information Institute (http://www.law.cornell.edu), which has an extensive collection of recent as well as landmark Supreme Court and other federal and state court decisions.

If you have the names of the parties involved in the case (e.g., *Brown v. Board of Education*), most legal databases have a search box for entering just the names of the parties.

If you have the legal citation (e.g., 410 U.S. 113), most legal databases have a search box for entering the legal citation.

If you have some information about a case (for example, a sexual harassment case at Wal-Mart), *always use secondary sources first to get additional information* (see below) before you try to track down the actual case in a legal database. A great deal of time can be wasted choosing specific court files to search only to find that the case you are looking for took place at a different level and jurisdiction. Your time might also be wasted by doing a general legal search in all court files and getting buried with too many similar types of cases.

If you are looking for cases on a legal topic, such as child custody, use secondary sources to find relevant cases rather than searching through the legal database of court decisions. Legal encyclopedias and law review articles, mentioned below, can be useful for topic searching.

USE SECONDARY SOURCES TO FIND RELATED CASES AND ANALYSIS ON POINTS OF LAW

Secondary sources such as newspaper articles, legal encyclopedia articles, law review or journal articles, or even books that cover the point of law (e.g., immigration) or a landmark case (*Muller v. Oregon*) can be useful to consult *before* looking for and reading the actual case you are studying. By reviewing secondary resources first, the researcher is better equipped to tackle the actual text of a court decision that is written in formal legal language. In addition, information from secondary sources will provide factual information that will aid in finding the case online.

Secondary sources include:

1. **Newspaper articles.** Large databases such as Newsbank and LexisNexis news file provide full text access to large numbers of newspapers. Searching these library-owned databases can be useful for getting background information about a case.

2. **Legal encyclopedias and** *American Law Reports.* Legal encyclopedias contain articles summarizing broad areas of law such as gun control or abortion. Each article provides citations to relevant cases, statutes, and other helpful materials. Legal encyclopedias are a great place to begin legal research. In addition to the titles listed below, well-known landmark cases can be found in *Great American Court Cases and Historic U.S. Court Cases, 1690–1990: An Encyclopedia.*

   American Law Reports (*ALR*) is available in print and online through the *Westlaw* database in some libraries. Articles focus on important legal topics and contain key citations to relevant cases, statutes, law review articles, and prevailing policy arguments.

   Corpus Juris Secundum (*CJS*) and *American Jurisprudence 2d* (*Am Jr 2d*) are the two main print legal encyclopedias in the United States. *Am Jr*

2d is also available on Westlaw. These encyclopedias provide article summaries on broad areas of law with citations to related cases.

Legal Research Encyclopedia is produced online by Cornell Law Library (http://www.lawschool.cornell.edu/lawlibrary/encyclopedia/). It provides a compilation of United States and international legal resources online and in print.

West's Encyclopedia to American Law is a research tool for a layperson with little knowledge of legal texts. It is national in scope and available in many libraries in print.

3. **Law review articles** are a good starting point for legal research as well as a place for analysis of case law and legal doctrine. Written by law students, professors, and lawyers, these articles pull together important cases and legal issues and can be searched by case as well as legal topic. The following are collections of law review articles or indexes to law review articles available by subscription at many academic libraries. The most comprehensive online collections are listed before the historical and print titles.

LexisNexis—Law Reviews files contain full-text law review and law journal articles from 1980 to the present.

Westlaw—Journals and Law Reviews file contains full-text law review and law journal articles from 1980 to the present.

Legaltrac is an online index to legal periodicals from 1980 to the present.

Hein-on-Line provides the full-text law journals and reviews from their inception through the present. It is a great resource for historical legal research.

Index to Legal Periodicals is a print index to law journals from 1908 to the present and is also available online with full text at some libraries.

Current Law Index is a comprehensive print index of law journals from 1980 to the present.

4. **Books.** Search the library online catalog to find information about the point of law or case you are researching. Search by case if it is famous, otherwise combine keyword terms such as:

field to search   **enter word/s to search**

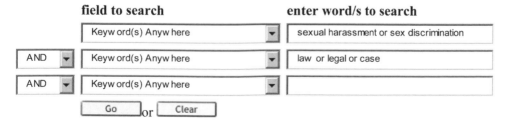

UNDERSTAND CITATIONS TO COURT CASES

Citations to case law are complicated because there are many different levels of courts ranging from county courts to the U.S. Supreme Court. In addition, each case can have parallel citations because commercial publishers use different numbering systems from the official government publication of a case. For example, the case of Teresa Harris against Forklift Systems can be cited three different ways depending on which publisher or online system is used to view the case:

Harris v. Forklift Sys, 510 U.S. 17 (1993)
Harris v. Forklift Sys, 126 L. Ed. 2d 295 (1993)
Harris v. Forklift Sys, 114 S. Ct. 367 (1993)

The first citation is the official version published by the U.S. government, the second and third are commercial editions—respectively, *Lawyers' Edition* published by Lawyers Cooperative Publishing and *Supreme Court Reporter* by West Publishing. All citations include the names of the parties, the volume number of the reporter, the abbreviation and starting page of the reporter, and the date.

The two accepted manuals for legal citation are *The Bluebook: A Uniform System of Citation* and the *ALWD Citation Manual: A Professional System of Citation*, which is used in many law schools. The two systems are very similar. Information on how to cite court cases, following the practices of these manuals, can be found at the Legal Information Institute at Cornell (www.law.cornell.edu/citation/).

USE A LEGAL DICTIONARY TO DECIPHER LEGAL TERMS

The most comprehensive and respected legal dictionary is *Black's Law Dictionary*. It is only available in print at this time. There are several free legal dictionaries on the web that are useful: *Merriam-Webster's Dictionary of Law* at http://dictionary.lp.findlaw.com/dictionary.html; and *Nolo's Legal Glossary* at http://www.nolo.com/glossary.cfm.

FIND SUPREME COURT CASES

The U.S. Supreme Court is the highest court in the United States. It is the final place for appeal because decisions at the Supreme Court level create legal precedents that guide lower courts and subsequent Supreme Court decisions. Each year thousands of cases make their way to the Supreme Court, but the Court only deals directly with a few hundred.

The majority of cases are dismissed and the ruling stands with the lower court.

The Supreme Court issues opinions and decisions indicating whether the Court upheld or reversed a lower court decision. The opinion provides an explanation of the legal reasoning used by the Court and a majority of the nine justices must agree on the decision. Sometimes justices choose to write separate opinions if they oppose the majority opinion, or if they are part of the majority but want to provide a different legal analysis of the decision.

Supreme Court opinions can be found online in the following free and library subscription databases. Subscription databases often provide more comprehensive coverage as well as annotations to related resources.

- LexisNexis provides the online version of the print *United States Supreme Court Reports* (Lawyers Edition and Lawyers Edition 2d). This database provides a comprehensive collection of Supreme Court decisions with links to related resources.
- Westlaw provides the online version of the *Supreme Court Reporter* beginning in 1882. This database provides a comprehensive collection of Supreme Court decisions with links to related resources.
- *United States Reports* (US) is the official record of Supreme Court decisions. It is available in print in many libraries.
- There are numerous free collections of Supreme Court decisions. The Legal Information Institute at Cornell (http://www.law.cornell.edu/) provides access to decisions from 1990 to the present as well as landmark court decisions and links to other decisions. FedWorld (http://www.fedworld.gov) provides pointers to various large academic collections of Supreme Court cases. Findlaw (http://www.findlaw.com) has a comprehensive collection from 1937 to present. Oyez, Oyez, Oyez (http://www.oyez.org/oyez/) provides audio oral arguments from the Supreme Court for all cases from 1995 to the present and selected cases prior to 1995.

FIND LOWER FEDERAL COURT CASES

United States Courts of Appeal (Circuit Courts)

The twelve U.S. courts of appeal are the intermediate appellate courts. Each court hears the appeals from the district courts in the group of states that fall within its circuit. In addition, the court of appeals for the federal circuit has special nationwide jurisdiction to hear federal cases, such as those involving international trade or patent laws. The decisions of these courts are final unless the Supreme Court reviews them. Decisions from the

U.S. courts of appeal are available in several commercial as well as free web sites. These courts also have their own home pages that provide information about the court, some decisions, and other publications.

- The *Federal Reporter*, also cited as *F* or *F 2d* or *F 3d*, is the commercial publisher for annotated circuit court decisions. It is available in print at law libraries and some research libraries.
- LexisNexis contains a comprehensive collection of circuit court decisions in the *Federal Case Law* file available online from some libraries.
- Westlaw contains a comprehensive collection of circuit court decisions under "Cases," available online from some libraries.
- The U.S. Courts web site (http://www.uscourts.gov) provides access to recent circuit court decisions. This tool is not as comprehensive as the commercial titles mentioned above.
- The Law Library of Congress (http://www.loc.gov/law/guide/usjudic.html) provides links to recent circuit court decisions and other federal court cases.

United States District Courts (Trial Courts)

The U.S. district courts are the federal trial–level courts of the federal court system. There are ninety-four federal judicial districts with a minimum of one in each state, some states having as many as four. Some district court decisions are published and can be found in the sources listed below.

- *Federal Supplement* (*F.Supp*) and *Federal Rules Decisions* (*FRD*) are the commercial annotated print copies of some decisions from the district courts and are available in some libraries.
- LexisNexis, available in many libraries, provides comprehensive access to district courts through the *Federal Case Law* file.
- Westlaw, available in many libraries, provides comprehensive access to district courts through the "Cases" section.
- Legal Information Institute (http://www.law.cornell.edu/federal/districts.html) provides some recent district court opinions and FindLaw (http://www.find law.org) provides links to web pages of district courts. Some of these web pages have decisions available.

FIND STATE COURT CASES

Each state has a court system that is structured similarly to the federal court system. These courts are located in cities and towns across the United States. State supreme and appellate court decisions can be found in commercial online databases. Partial state court collections of decisions are available on court web sites.

- LexisNexis, available in many libraries, provides access to state supreme court cases and appellate-level decisions. Dates vary by state.
- Westlaw, available in many libraries, provides access to state supreme court cases and appellate-level decisions. Dates vary by state.
- FindLaw (http://www.findlaw.com) and the Legal Information Institute (http://www.law.cornell.edu/citation/) provide access to some recent state court decisions. Dates vary by state.

DETERMINE WHETHER A CASE IS STILL "GOOD LAW"

Two commercial online publishers of legal information provide special systems to determine if a law is still "good law" (i.e., whether a particular case still has value as precedent or has been affected by a later court decision or legislative action). This is called "Shepardizing" in LexisNexis and "KeyCite" in Westlaw. Using either of these systems allows the legal researcher to:

- find out if an established rule of law might later have been reversed or modified on appeal;
- determine how many times a case has been cited by other cases and whether later decisions have followed the precedent set or reversed it;
- locate other cases and law review articles that deal with the same point of law.

LexisNexis provides Shepardizing, named after the publisher of the original print volumes that created this service. In LexisNexis, Shepardizing can be done for Supreme Court cases only. Westlaw provides a citator service called KeyCite, which covers all cases, including unpublished opinions and selected administrative decisions. In order to use either KeyCite or Shepard's, the researcher starts with a known case. Both LexisNexis and Westlaw have help screens that guide the researcher through the citator process.

CRITICALLY EVALUATE LEGAL RESOURCES

Legal resources can be broken down into two types of resources for purposes of evaluation—primary and secondary.

Primary documents—such as the text of a Supreme Court case—can often be taken at face value provided the text is a reliable authentic copy.

Use a legal database such as LexisNexis or Westlaw to ensure that the case is an authentic and accurate copy. Avoid using web pages that post the text of one or a few particular cases. Sometimes these cases are only reproduced in part or not carefully copied or checked for accuracy.

Secondary documents—such as law review articles, books, newspapers, magazines, or encyclopedia articles—need to undergo a more careful evaluation process. The most important issue is to determine whether a resource is scholarly or popular. Use scholarly sources, such as law review articles, whenever possible. If the topic is extremely current, use published sources, such as legal newspapers or other newspapers or magazines, before relying on blogs or web pages.

Law review and other journal articles undergo a process of peer review. This means that editors' decisions about whether or not to publish a paper are based on the judgments of experts—other scholars in the same field—who review the manuscript prior to publication. Reviewers' comments serve to keep poorly constructed research out of journals and provide valuable feedback and corrections to authors. The authors then make changes and improve the quality of the article being published. Some peer review is "blind," meaning reviewers do not know the identity of the author they are reviewing. This prevents the review from being colored by any prior assumptions a reviewer might have about a particular author's work.

The following criteria will assist you in determining the scholarly value of secondary legal resources such as articles and books.

Determine Purpose and Scholarly Nature

What is the purpose of the article or book? Was it written to further knowledge and research about a particular topic, or was it written to entertain or persuade? Determine the intended audience. Was the piece written for other scholars, educated laypeople, or for the general public?

Some clues for determining whether an article is scholarly include:

- the level and tone of the language,
- the length—scholarly articles can run ten to twenty pages,
- an extensive bibliography of reputable sources,
- an indication that research was conducted and conclusions were drawn—not a simple report of events,
- an author who is a professor or expert in the field,
- little, if any, advertising,
- an indication that a scholarly press, scholarly society, or academic institute published the article.

Evaluate Authority

Authority refers to the credentials of both the author and the publisher or sponsor of a journal, magazine, or newspaper. Scholarly journal articles often contain a sentence at the beginning or end of the article listing at minimum the author's institutional affiliation. Magazines sometimes provide a sentence about the credentials of the freelancer or journalist writing the article. Do a Google search to find the author's web page or check a journal database to see if the author has published other articles on the subject. Authors writing for law review journals are usually advanced law students, law professors, or lawyers. Authors writing for magazines and newspapers are journalists who typically do not have in-depth expertise in a particular area.

Find out the publisher of the journal, magazine, or newspaper article. If there is not a clear publisher listed, the article may be self-published on the web. This means it may not have gone through an editorial or peer-review process. A scholarly journal article can be published by a scholarly society or a commercial publisher. It will have an editor and editorial board of some sort, as well as an established submission and review procedure that is explained on the publisher's web site or at the front of a print copy of the journal.

Determine Possible Bias

Scholarly journal articles strive to present research that is accurate and free of bias. No article is completely objective, but the peer-review and editorial processes that scholarly publishers use filter out articles that do not adhere to good research standards and approved methodologies. Scholarly law articles provide extensive bibliographies that link the work of one author to the research that has already been reported and to important case law and statutes. No scholarly work is written in a vacuum—each article acknowledges how new research connects to earlier studies.

Many newspapers and magazines have a framework or belief system that influences what they print. A newspaper such as the *New York Times* has a strong commitment to objective and accurate reporting. The newspaper attempts to balance both conservative and liberal viewpoints on its editorial pages, and also attempts to report on all sides of an issue. While some media watchdogs feel the paper is not objective enough, a letters-to-the-editor section provides an outlet for opposing views. Thinking about the audience for a particular publication will assist you in determining if there is a strong agenda for that publication. Legal newsletters and newspapers sometimes have a political slant, and even though what they report is factually accurate, they may present issues in a particular light.

Use Multiple Sources

For any argument you make that is controversial, try to have more than one citation to an article that backs up your statements. If you can only find one article that supports your ideas, be suspicious, especially if the source is unpublished.

Investigate Accuracy, Consistency, and Content

Determining accuracy involves viewing the article with a critical eye. Look for external consistency. Does the content seem to jibe with other research findings on the topic? Check also for internal consistency. Are the arguments that are being made supported within the work itself? Does the work seem plausible? Are statements backed up by citations to other research? Is the bibliography substantial and does it cite scholarly or popular sources? Determine whether the author has clearly stated a hypothesis, related the article to previous research, and interpreted the results correctly. Look for any discrepancies between the results and the hypothesis.

Note Currency

For some research the currency of an article is important. In legal research make sure to locate any recent research or analysis that has been done on a case or point of law.

Determine Relevance

Decide whether the article directly relates to your research topic. Determine if the information in the article supports or refutes arguments you are trying to put forward. It is often tempting to include information that is interesting or exciting, but it may not further the goals of your research paper. When collecting resources to use for your paper, compare each source to the other sources you have gathered. Does one particular source add anything to the research you are presenting? What is the relative value of the source in question?

Examine Your Assumptions

Every researcher begins a project with some assumptions or hypotheses. It is important to put aside your own ideas as you gather and read articles on your topic. Ignoring articles that refute your hypothesis will not serve you in the long run. You must connect your ideas to previous research. Be open to adjusting your own set of beliefs about a topic as you digest the current research. It is acceptable to use articles to bolster your own arguments, but if there is substantial research out there that presents an alternative view, you must acknowledge and respond to it.

NOTES

1. *St. Clair v. Johnny's Oyster & Shrimp Inc.*, 76. Supp. 2d 773 (S.D. Tex. 1999).
2. Ibid.

REFERENCES

McDonough, Molly. 2004. In Google we trust? *ABA Journal* 90, no. 10:30.

7

United States Government Documents and Statistics

Mr. Kissinger asked: "Can we tell them no? When I talked to the president, he was loaded."

Elizabeth Becker, "Kissinger Tapes," 2004

Government documents provide an enormous variety of primary and secondary source material that can foster our understanding of the past as well as provide information on current policies and decision-making. Government documents can be defined as anything produced by a government entity or with government funds. They can include Executive Orders issued by the president, statistics collected by the Bureau of the Census, as well as songs, scraps of paper, and oral histories. They can also consist of declassified documents released under the Freedom of Information Act, including the above quotation, which states that President Nixon was too drunk to talk with the prime minister of Great Britain regarding the eruption of the Arab-Israeli War of 1973.

Government documents can provide historical detail to further our understanding of the conditions during the women's rights movement at the beginning of the twentieth century.

In a 1913 report to the Senate titled "The Mission of Woman," Albert Taylor Bledsoe argued that equal rights would destroy marriage and lead to a significant drop in the birth rate. Bledsoe stated that all women's rights advocates would be destined to be spinsters because no man is interested in marrying a strong-minded woman. (U.S. Congress, Senate 1913)

Classified government documents released under the Freedom of Information Act can provide insights on recent covert operations.

In the case of torture used by the U.S. in Abu Ghraib prison in Baghdad, questions were raised about whether this was the work of an isolated few or a more systemic practice. According to documents acquired by the Baltimore Sun in 1997, the CIA's "Human Resource Exploitation Training Manual" provided instructions for using torture as late as the 1980s. While Congress investigated the matter and CIA manuals were revised to denounce the use of torture, the techniques used at Abu Ghraib bore a strong similarity to the methods discussed in the CIA manual *prior* to its revision. (Matthews 2004)

Government documents can also provide us with useful statistics and information relating to health, education, crime, computer security, terrorism, transportation, and almost any topic imaginable. But research involving government documents can be complicated because the U.S. government is the largest producer of information in the world, and the information is produced in a decentralized and nonstandardized way. Close to six thousand agencies within the federal government produce their own information independently with little collaboration (Robinson 1998).

Over time, attempts have been made to pull together the vast array of government documents with varying degrees of success. This chapter provides information on how to search for government documents using specialized search engines, meta-sites, and indexes. Print sources sometimes must be used to locate historical documents, though more of these sources are migrating to the web. Separate techniques are explained for finding presidential, legislative, and statistical documents. Judicial documents, court cases, and other legal research resources are covered in chapter six. Critical evaluation, covered at the end of this chapter, is a crucial step in using government documents for research. Scholars generally view government publications as reliable and objective, but in some cases information might be distorted by political agendas, bias, or the particular goals of the issuing agency.

FIND FEDERAL AGENCY DOCUMENTS

Finding government documents generated by federal agencies involves several possible strategies:

- Use a specialized search engine or index.
- Go to the web site of the agency producing the information needed.
- Use historical indexes to locate older government documents.

Use a *Specialized* Search Engine to Locate Agency Documents

Using Google or another large search engine *can* help you find a government document you are seeking when you have the exact title or other

precise information about a specific document. However, if you are looking for documents about a particular topic, such as discrimination in the
workplace, using a search engine that focuses on government documents
will be more effective.

GPO Access

http://www.gpoaccess.gov
Run by the Government Printing Office, *GPO Access* is a portal to government
documents on the web. This site provides access to specialized agency databases
and has the ability to search across many agencies by broad subject category. In
addition, this site provides access to the *Catalog of U.S. Government Publications*
mentioned directly below.

Catalog of U.S. Government Publications (Government Printing Office [GPO])

http://www.gpoaccess.gov/cgp/index.html
The *Catalog* is a free index to many federal agency–produced publications from
1994 to the present. Whenever possible the index record links to the full text of
the document online.

GPO Monthly Catalog

This title is the library subscription version of the *Catalog* mentioned directly above.
It indexes government documents from 1976 to the present.

FedWorld/National Technical Information Service (NTIS)

http://www.ntis.gov
NTIS is the largest resource for government-funded scientific, technical, engineering, and business-related information available. *FedWorld* is the NTIS gateway that
provides access to these unclassified technical reports.

Google's Uncle Sam

http://www.google.com/unclesam
Google's *Uncle Sam* searches federal and state government documents on the web
using Google's search technology but limiting the search to government web sites.
Not all government documents on the web can be found with Google because many
are located in the "deep web" (i.e., buried down several layers on a web page or
in a database that Google is unable to reach).

WorldCat (Online Computer Library Center)

WorldCat combines the holdings of library online catalogs from around the country and from other countries as well. Because many libraries have cataloged the
government documents the libraries own, *WorldCat* provides a sophisticated search
engine for government documents. *WorldCat* is able to provide a deeper level of
access to documents that Google cannot find. Once a document is located in

WorldCat, an interlibrary loan can be requested from your library web page so that you can borrow the document.

In addition to the general tools listed above, there are a number of specialized databases that provide access to documents issued in particular subject areas. The more popular ones include *PubMed* (medicine), *ERIC* (education), *Agricola* (agriculture, plant, and animal science), and the Library of Congress *American Memory Project* (history).

Use a Search Engine to Locate a Specific Agency

Many known government agencies can be found by searching Google. If you do not know the name of the agency that covers the topic you are researching, use FirstGov (www.firstgov.gov), the official web portal of the U.S. government. FirstGov provides searches by topic across government web sites.

Find Historical Federal Agency Documents

Older documents, often in print form, can be found at government-designated depository libraries. Many documents released prior to 1990, unless they are particularly noteworthy, are only available in print. *The Monthly Catalog of United States Government Publications* indexes documents from 1895 to the present and is available in many libraries. If you seek documents printed prior to 1895, there are two publications that index agency documents—Benjamin Perley Poore's 1885 title, *A Descriptive Catalogue of the Government Publications of the United States*; and John Griffith Ames's 1905 title, *Comprehensive Index to the Publications of the United States Government*. Finding older documents not listed in these indexes can be a complex process. Consult a government documents reference librarian for assistance.

FIND PRESIDENTIAL INFORMATION SOURCES

Presidential documents include Executive Orders, reprieves and pardons, speeches and statements, treaties, appointments to office, vetoes of acts of Congress, updates on the state of the union, and proposed legislation.

Many other documents produced by the president, including both personal and official papers, are sealed from the public for a period of time. Many of these documents are not immediately released because they might include national secrets or classified information. Unlike the works of Congress and the Supreme Court, much of what the president does is kept confidential until after leaving office. Presidential papers after 1900 are archived in presidential libraries and for the most part are available for scholars to use. Earlier presidential documents were considered personal property and are more difficult to locate, though partial collections have been microfilmed and are available in some research libraries.

Use Executive Branch Web Sites to Locate Information

FirstGov Federal Executive Branch
www.firstgov.gov/Agencies/Federal/Executive.shtml
FirstGov.gov is the official gateway to U.S. government information. The "Federal Executive Branch" section provides access to the president's radio addresses, major speeches, policies on important issues, appointments and nominations, and recent press releases.

GPO Access—Executive Branch Resources
www.gpoaccess.gov/executive.html
This site provides official electronic versions of many current and historical presidential documents.

The White House
www.whitehouse.gov
This site provides access to current presidential documents, including major speeches of the current president, presidential appointments, news, press briefings, policies, and biographical information. The goal of this site is to foster a positive image of the president and his policies; it does not provide comprehensive information, and additional resources need to be consulted to gain a full picture.[1]

Find Executive Orders, Presidential Messages, Proclamations, and Other Documents Issued by the President

Executive Orders are one of the oldest types of presidential directives (Hernon, Relyea, Dugan, and Cheverie 2002). They began with George Washington but were not numbered until 1862. In 1935 Congress required that all Executive Orders be published in the *Federal Register* and from that time on they have been collected in Title 3 of the *Code of Federal Regulations*. Executive Orders from 1862 to 1938 can be found in *Presidential Executive Orders* (Lord 1944). Directives emanating from the National Security Council are kept secret, though directives issued prior to 1960 are now being declassified and are available through the National Archives via presidential libraries. Many other types of presidential statements such as administrative orders, designations of officials, announcements, military orders, and proclamations can be found in one or more of the sources listed below.

Weekly Compilation of Presidential Documents
www.gpoaccess.gov/wcomp
This title contains the text of speeches, statements, communications to Congress, Executive Orders, news conferences, and proclamations made by the president during the previous week. It is available prior to 1993 in print (SuDocs* AE 2.10) and from 1993 to the present online.

Federal Register
http://www.gpoaccess.gov/fr
Started in 1936, the *Federal Register* contains Executive Orders, presidential proclamations, and proposed agency regulations. It is also available through LexisNexis Congressional Universe at many libraries.

Title 3 of the *Code of Federal Regulations*
www.gpoaccess.gov/cfr
Title 3 contains Executive Orders, proclamations, and other significant documents. The paper version is available from 1936 to the present in many libraries. Documents from 1996 to the present are online.

Public Papers of the President
This print title available in many libraries provides an official record of the papers of Hoover, Truman, Eisenhower, Kennedy, Johnson, Nixon, Ford, Carter, Reagan, Bush (Sr.), Clinton, and Bush (George W.). Reagan, Clinton, and Bush (George W.) papers are also available through the National Archives (www.archives.gov). Microfilm collections contain what is available of the papers of twenty of the country's earliest presidents. This collection is accessed in many research libraries by searching the name of the president as a title followed by "papers" (e.g., "James Madison Papers").

Find Federal Budgetary Information

The Budget of the United States
www.gpoaccess.gov/usbudget/index.html

---

*SuDocs stands for "Superintendent of Documents" number. It is the classification system used by the U.S. government and libraries that house government documents. It is based on pulling together documents by their issuing body and type. For example all congressional hearings are given a SuDocs number that begins with Y4.

The budget contains an overview of departmental and agency budgets as well as specific agency and program appropriations. It is available in print at most libraries (SuDoc PREX 2.8) as well as online from 1997 to the present.

Economic Report of the President
www.gpoaccess.gov/eop/index.html
This title provides an overview of the economy and an analysis of current issues. It includes charts and graphs and provides an overview of a particular administration's economic policy. This title is available in print at many libraries and is also online from 1995 to present.

Locate Information in Presidential Libraries

The past eleven presidents now have presidential libraries operating through the National Archives and Records Administration (www.archives. gov/presidential_libraries). Some material located in these libraries is available online though most remains accessible only by visiting the library. The Library of Congress *American Memory Project* contains a selection of papers for earlier presidents.

Locate Foreign Relations Documents

Foreign relations are conducted in conjunction with the executive branch of the government. The Department of State issues official records of its work through the U.S. *Department of State Dispatch* as well as press releases through its web site. Historical coverage of foreign policy primary sources is available through *Foreign Relations of the United States.*

U.S. Department of State Dispatch
http://dosfan.lib.uic.edu/ERC/briefing/dispatch/
This title overviews foreign policy, provides reprints of speeches and congressional testimony of the president and secretary of state, and contains policy statements and profiles of other countries. It is available in print (SuDoc S 1.3/5) and can be found online from 1990 to 1996 (http://dosfan.lib.uic.edu/ERC/briefing/dispatch/index.html). Its predecessor was the *Department of State Bulletin*, which was the official record of U.S. foreign policy from 1939 to 1989 (SuDoc S 1.3). Press briefings and news releases are also available from the State Department web site (www.state.gov).

Foreign Relations of the United States
This title contains the historical record of foreign policy and diplomatic relations. The annual volumes provide background documents such as diplomatic communications, memoranda, notes, and other primary sources tracing U.S. foreign policy.

Declassification procedures mandate a twenty-five-year time lag for release of these documents, making this source useful for historical foreign policy research. Volumes from 1943 to the most recently released are available online through www.state.gov. In addition, *American Foreign Policy: Current Documents* (Sudoc JX 1417 .A43) provides contemporary foreign policy primary source materials.

Find Declassified Documents

Many government publications are withheld from public view by classifying them as "Top Secret," "Secret," or "Confidential." Periodic reviews of classification procedures have found that too many government documents are classified and remain classified for lengthy periods of time. In 1995 the Clinton Administration signed an Executive Order that required declassification of materials that are more than twenty-five years old and declassification of recently classified information after a period of 10 years. However, portions of this order have recently been weakened by the Bush administration (Milbank and Allen 2003). Though it is beyond the scope of this book to provide detailed resources on finding declassified materials, many good resources are available on the web, including:

University of California, Berkeley, Libraries
http://www.lib.berkeley.edu/doemoff/gov_decldoc.html
Declassified Government Documents Guide

The National Security Archive via George Washington University
http://www.gwu.edu/~nsarchiv/

The Freedom of Information Act provides a formal procedure for requesting government documents that are classified. It is now used regularly by scholars and journalists to gain more access to the historical record. Information about this procedure can be found at the National Security Archive listed directly above.

FIND LEGISLATIVE INFORMATION

Legislative information consists of the documents and publications generated or used by Congress in the process of making laws. The Congress of the United States consists of two houses, the Senate and the House of Representatives, as well as a number of supporting agencies such as the Congressional Research Service, the General Accounting Office, and the Congressional Budget Office.

There are four types of legislation that pass through Congress, with bills being the most common type. Thousands of bills are introduced each year but only about five percent are enacted into law. The remaining bills die at the end of a congressional session. As the bills make their way through the two houses of Congress, documents are generated that provide both analysis and legislative intent of the subject matter of the bill. Scholars and policy-makers use these documents to study the work of Congress and the issues that are considered by this rule-making body of government.

THOMAS, from the Library of Congress and GPO Access from the Government Printing Office are the key web sites providing free legislative documents. In addition, *LexisNexis Congressional* is the primary library subscription service providing access to legislative documents. This subscription service, along with Westlaw (for laws in their final form), provides superior searching mechanisms, indexing, and annotations that the government web sites often lack.

Understand How a Bill Becomes a Law

It is vital to understand how a bill becomes a law in order to track legislative documents. The following is a list of the most typical steps a bill goes through to become a law, followed by the documents generated at that stage. For a more detailed treatment see *United States Government Information* (Hernon, Relyea, Dugan, and Cheverie 2002) or "How Congress Makes Laws" available at Thomas.loc.gov.

1. The bill is introduced on the floor of the House or Senate. It is assigned to one or more committees.

Documents generated:

- Text of bill
- Name of committee(s) that will work on the bill

2. The committee or a subcommittee holds a hearing and/or commissions a study related to the bill.

Documents generated:

- Committee hearings
- Study sometimes published as a committee print

3. If a committee approves a bill it issues a report to the House or Senate.

Documents generated:

- Committee reports

4. The bill is debated on the floor of the House or Senate and a vote is taken. If the vote is positive, the bill is referred to the other chamber of Congress and the above steps are repeated.

(continued)

Documents generated:

- Text of debate and voting record

5. A Conference Committee is held if the House and Senate pass differing versions of the bill.

Documents generated:

- Conference report
- Final vote

6. The bill is signed, vetoed, or not acted upon by the president. If not acted upon, it becomes law in ten days.

Documents generated:

- Statement president makes when signing or vetoing

7. The law is entered into the record.

Documents generated:

- Published law (called a Public Law or Statute or Act)
- Integration (codification) of law into current legal code

Find a Bill

There are four different types of resolutions: bills, joint resolutions, concurrent resolutions, and simple resolutions. Bills are the most common form in which legislation is introduced. Most bills that are introduced will die by the end of the congressional term in which they were introduced, but some of these same bills, sometimes revised, will be reintroduced the following year and assigned new bill numbers. To become a law a bill must pass both houses of Congress and be approved or not acted on by the president. If the president vetoes a bill, Congress must override the veto by two-thirds of both houses.

The summary, status, and in some cases, the text of a bill can be found in the following:

- THOMAS (Thomas.loc.gov); 1973 to present
- GPO Access (www.gpoaccess.gov); 1993 to present
- LexisNexis (library subscription); 1989 to present
- For the text of bills not available online, use the *Congressional Record* in print and available in many libraries.

Find the Committee(s) Working on the Bill

A bill is assigned to one or more congressional committees. The committee investigates and decides whether to recommend passage of the bill. The assignment to committee is recorded in the *Congressional Record*, which is discussed in detail under "Find Congressional Debates." Knowing the committee name will assist you in tracking documents if you are using the free government web sites.

Find a Hearing

Committees frequently hold hearings on a proposed bill for a variety of reasons, including political motivations and fact-finding missions. Hearings can provide meaty information about a particular piece of legislation. They include verbatim testimony from witnesses as well as documents submitted by interested parties. Interest groups and experts testify and insert letters, documents, reports, statistics, and studies that are then published with the text of the hearing. In addition to testimonies from many experts, the testimonies of Gary Cooper, Walt Disney, Jackie Robinson, Mark Twain (Robinson 1998), Richard Gere, Julia Roberts, and Jessica Lange can be found in congressional hearings.

There are several techniques for finding hearings. Once you locate the title of a hearing using the resources below, check for a link. If there is no link to the full text, you can find many hearings in print and in government depository libraries under their SuDoc number.

- *CIS Index*, available by library subscription online in *LexisNexis Congressional* or in print provides full-text hearings from 1993 to the present (online version only), and indexing for hearings from 1789 to the present.
- THOMAS (Thomas.loc.gov) provides some full-text hearings by committee from 1997 to the present. No index is available.
- GPO Access (www.gpoaccess.gov) provides selected hearings by committee from 1995 to the present. No index is available.

Find a Committee Print

Committees sometimes commission a background research report called a committee print on proposed legislation. Committee research staff, the Congressional Research Service, or outside consultants prepare these studies. Committee prints often contain valuable information, including authoritative historical background information, statistics, and analysis.

- *CIS Index*, available by library subscription through *LexisNexis Congressional*, provides indexing from 1970 to the present and some selected full text from 1993 to the present.
- *CIS U.S. Congressional Committee Prints Index* provides indexing from 1830 to 1969 in print. Some libraries have also purchased the companion microfilm set of full-text committee prints.
- GPO Access (www.gpoaccess.gov) has committee prints for the current session only.

Find a Committee Report

When a bill is "reported from committee" for consideration by the larger body, the report is usually favorable, but occasionally a committee will write an unfavorable report. The most common scenario is that no report is issued and the bill dies at the end of the congressional term. Committee reports sometimes contain analysis, the committee's rationale for recommending passage, issues raised in closed hearings, cost projections, and minority views, in addition to the text of the proposed legislation.

- *CIS Index*, available by library subscription through *LexisNexis Congressional*, provides indexing from 1970 to the present and full text from 1989 to the present.
- THOMAS (Thomas.loc.gov) provides reports from 1995 to present.
- GPO Access (www.gpoaccess.gov) provides reports from 1995 to the present.
- The *United States Congressional Serial Set*, usually referred to as the *Serial Set* is available at many libraries in print from 1817 to the present. Selected documents from this set are available from the Library of Congress (http://lcweb2.loc.gov/ammem/amlaw). There are several indexes to this large collection of books, including the *U.S. Serial Set Index*. Documents before 1838 can be found in *American State Papers*, which covers congressional documents from 1789 to 1838, and is available at the Library of Congress (http://lcweb2.loc.gov/ammem/amlaw/) as well as in print.

Find Congressional Debates

Congressional debates have been recorded in the *Congressional Record* since 1789. These discussions provide scholars with information about the legislative intent behind a particular piece of legislation. The *Congressional Record* serves as a verbatim account of what has been said on the floor of Congress on a particular day or what a legislator requests be inserted into the record. In the past, senators and representatives were able to "correct" information that was recorded in the *Congressional*

Record. When reviewing text in order to correct misspellings, some legislators took the liberty of altering their remarks after the fact. Recent rules have limited the ability of legislators to alter the content of what was said on the floor.

The *Congressional Record* also includes voting records, legislative actions, and the full text of many bills. In addition to being available in the *Congressional Record*, debate on the floor of Congress is televised, broadcast live on CSPAN, and archived by the Library of Congress.

- The full text of the *Congressional Record* is available by library subscription from 1985 to the present in *LexisNexis Congressional*.
- The *Congressional Record* is available in print or microform from 1789 to the present in many libraries. A separate index, the *Congressional Record Index* is also available at many libraries.
- The *Congressional Record* is available for free on THOMAS (Thomas.loc.gov) from 1989 to the present.
- Some historical issues of the *Congressional Record* and its predecessors, *Annals of Congress, Register of Debates*, and *Congressional Globe* are available online at the Library of Congress (http://lcweb2.loc.gov/ammem/amlaw/).

Find a Public Law

Once a bill becomes a law it is assigned a number based on the number of the Congress in which it passed (e.g., 2003-4 would indicate the 108th Congress) followed by a chronological number (e.g., 108-4 would be the fourth law passed by the 108th Congress). Many laws are also referred to by their popular name, such as the "Clean Air Act."

Public laws are available in a collection called the *Statutes at Large* that contains the exact text of all the laws that were passed each year, in the order in which they were passed. They are "at large," meaning the text of each law is kept separate from the next. After a law is passed, it is codified (integrated) into the *United States Code*. For example, if a new law were passed instituting harsher penalties for drunk driving, the text of the law would be listed in the *Statutes at Large*. But pieces of this new law would be inserted into the law that is currently in effect—the *U.S. Code*—wherever it impacted current law, in some cases modifying or adding to the text that was there before. The *Code* is a living document that is constantly being updated with the passage of new laws.

The *U.S. Code* is the official version of the current "law of the land," but many scholars use annotated versions such as the *United States Code Annotated* (part of the Westlaw database) or the *United States Code Service* (part of LexisNexis). These commercial versions are updated faster than the official version and also add extra material that ties particular laws to relevant court cases, law review articles, and regulations.

The *Statutes at Large* (the text of the law as passed) can be accessed using the following resources:

- GPO Access (www.gpoaccess.gov) provides laws from 1995 to the present.
- The *Statutes at Large* is available in many libraries in print.
- *LexisNexis Congressional* provides laws from 1988 to the present and is available from the "Databases" page of many research libraries.
- THOMAS (Thomas.loc.gov) provides laws from 1989 to the present and summaries from 1973 to the present.

The *U.S. Code* (the laws that are currently in effect) can be accessed using the following resources:

- The Office of the Law Revision Council is the official publisher of the *U.S. Code* and provides the *Code* online at http://uscode.house.gov/lawrevision counsel.shtml.
- The Legal Information Institute at Cornell (http://www4.law.cornell.edu/ uscode/topn/) provides links from the popular names of laws to their sections in the *Code*.
- Westlaw provides access to the *United States Code Annotated*. It is available in some research libraries and provides helpful annotations in addition to the text of the *Code*.
- *LexisNexis Congressional* provides access to the *United States Code Service*. It is available in some research libraries and provides helpful annotations in addition to the text of the *Code*.

Trace the Legislative History of a Law

Tracing a legislative history involves finding and analyzing the documents that led to a specific law being passed. Laws are often broad and general, and it is important to determine the legislative intent behind a particular law being passed. Scholars, lawyers, and policy-makers compile legislative histories in order to interpret and apply the law. Because most bills never become law, tracing the history of a law usually involves working backward from the law to the initial bill.

The easiest way to trace the history of a law is to find out if another source has already completed the task. Legislative histories for laws passed after 1970 are available on *CIS Index*, which is available online in the LexisNexis database or in print in many libraries. The *CIS Index* will provide a list of the relevant documents and in some cases the full text of those documents. For laws passed before 1970, use the sources listed above in the section on "Finding Legislative Information" to track down the relevant hearings, committee prints, and other congressional documents; or use *Sources of Compiled Legislative Histories: A Bibliography of Government Documents, Periodical Articles, and Books* (Johnson 1979). Secondary sources such as journal articles in politics, public policy and law, or newspapers and magazines can also be used to gather more information about the passage of a law. The *National Journal* provides background information and news regarding legislative activities. The *Journal* is available at most libraries. (To find articles see chapter 3.)

Use Congressional Agencies to Gather Documentation

Congressional Research Service

The Congressional Research Service works for Congress. This team of researchers provides nonpartisan in-depth policy analysis, legal research, legislative histories, and answers to thousands of reference questions from Congress. Some of their work is not available to the public, but access to some reports can be found at the House Committee on Rules (www.house.gov/rules/crs_reports.htm), at other congressional committee web sites, and at www.opencrs.com. Because there are no copyright issues with these government-funded documents, a Google search combining your topic with "Congressional Research Service" will sometimes turn up relevant reports. Sometimes legislators are willing to provide a constituent with a report when asked. Some research libraries own reports from 1991 to the present, and the Penny Hill Press sells copies of reports to individuals through www.pennyhill.com.

General Accounting Office

The General Accounting Office (www.gao.gov) is considered the "watchdog" arm of Congress. This office oversees the spending of public funds, performs investigations and audits, and issues reports on its findings. These reports provide deep analysis on a broad range of topics and can be found on the office's website from 1995 to the present. Older reports are available in print in many libraries.

Congressional Budget Office

Created in 1974, the Congressional Budget Office provides Congress with objective nonpartisan analysis needed for economic and budgetary decisions. Publications, economic analysis, and briefs can be found at their web site (www.cbo.gov).

Find Historical Congressional Documents using the *U.S. Serial Set*

There are many ways to do historical research on the work of Congress. The *U.S. Serial Set* is one of the most frequently used sources for historical research. This work, available in many libraries, began in 1789 and continues in print today. It includes House and Senate reports and documents as well as other materials ordered printed by Congress (including presidential messages to Congress and special reports and background information given to Congress). Several indexes for the *U.S. Serial Set* exist, including the *CIS U.S. Serial Set Index* (in print as well as on *LexisNexis Congressional Historical Indexes*, available online at some libraries). In addition, early documents are available at the Library of Congress from the *Continental Congress and the Constitutional Convention, 1774–1789* (http://memory.loc.gov/ammem/bdsds/bdsdhome.html) and *A Century of Lawmaking for a New Nation: U.S. Congressional Documents and Debates* (http://memory.loc.gov/ammem/amlaw/lawhome.html).

FIND GOVERNMENT DOCUMENTS FROM OTHER COUNTRIES AND RESOURCES FROM INTERGOVERNMENTAL ORGANIZATIONS

Government documents from other countries, as well as reports from intergovernmental organizations such as the United Nations, can provide rich primary source materials for any research project that focuses on countries beyond the United States.

Three institutions provide comprehensive meta-sites to foreign government document collections.

- Columbia University Libraries
  http://www.columbia.edu/cu/lweb/indiv/lehman/guides/countries.html
- Northwestern University Libraries
  http://www.library.northwestern.edu/govpub/resource/internat/foreign.html
- University of Michigan Libraries
  http://www.lib.umich.edu/govdocs/foreign.html

Intergovernmental organizations issue a wide variety of reports, press releases, and other publications. Information resources issued by organizations such as the United Nations, the International Labour Organization, the World Bank, OECD, and others can be accessed through the following web sites. Much of this information is free, though some commercial databases owned by libraries provide more comprehensive and better organized access to these resources. Both free and library subscription databases can be found on these meta-sites.

- Northwestern University Libraries
  http://www.library.northwestern.edu/govpub/resource/internat/igo.html
- Duke University Libraries
  http://docs.lib.duke.edu/igo/subject.html

CRITICALLY EVALUATE GOVERNMENT DOCUMENTS

Government documents present unique challenges in terms of reliability. Their diversity dictates that researchers use a variety of evaluation strategies. Some government documents, provided they pass the test of authenticity (i.e., they really are what they purport to be), can be taken at face value, such as:

- the text of a Supreme Court opinion;
- the transcript of a congressional hearing;
- the text of a statute or regulation.

Other government documents need further analysis. A report on dietary recommendations that draws on data from the food industry should be interpreted cautiously. For the most part government documents and reports are viewed as reliable and have gone through some degree of vetting. Documents such as those produced by the Congressional Research Service have a reputation for being nonpartisan and objective. Similarly, the U.S. State Department's *Country Reports on Human Rights Practices* are well respected by researchers in the field of human rights.

Due to their authority and public nature, government documents are subject to a great deal of scrutiny so that questionable research is often brought to light. Recently, sixty scientists, including twenty Nobel laureates, released a report charging a "well-established pattern of suppression and distortion of scientific findings by high-ranking Bush Administration political appointees across numerous federal agencies" (Union of Concerned Scientists 2004). The report stated that unqualified political appointees were assigned to panels advising policymakers on areas including reproductive health and childhood lead-poisoning prevention. In one incident the government admitted to improperly altering a report that directly contradicted research findings (National Council for Research on Women 2004).

Government documents need to be individually evaluated using common sense and knowledge about the background and authority of a particular document. In addition, there are general principles, listed below, that can be used to help evaluate any document. When reviewing government documents, special attention needs to be paid to *why* a government document was produced and the perceived audience for the document. Hidden agendas and issues of bias and authority need to be investigated carefully.

The following criteria can be used in evaluating government documents.

Determine Authenticity

Determine if the work is authentic. If the government document is on the web, does it have a government URL ending in ".gov" or ".mil" (for military)? Sometimes government documents are reproduced in part or interpreted on other web sites. Try to find the original document and not a copy reproduced and possibly changed by someone else.

Check for External Consistency and Use Multiple Sources

Compare the document to other information on the same subject. If at all possible, compare the document to published sources such as magazines, newspapers, books, or journal articles. These publications have been vetted by editors and fact-checkers. In some cases the publications have been reviewed by experts in the field and can help you verify that the information in the government document is accurate. Use the knowledge you are accumulating from all that you have read on the subject to determine if the document seems accurate.

Examine Motivation of Author or Organization

Try to determine the motivation of the author or government agency that produced the document. What was the reason for the document's being produced? Who was the audience for the document? What was the social, political, and economic context in which the document was created? Documents produced by the Congressional Research Service have a reputation for being nonpartisan and objective. They are produced to help legislators evaluate issues from all sides, and researchers usually feel the documents can be relied upon. On the other hand, independent scientists have been critical of some reports by the Environmental Protection Agency. For example, a press release issued shortly after the September 11th terrorist attacks was heavily edited by the National Security Council, which deleted concerns about air quality for New Yorkers and provided reassurance in order to ensure a return to normalcy (Pope 2004).

Note Researcher Bias

Keep in mind your own biases. What do you bring to the reading of the document? You are interpreting the document based on your own life experiences and beliefs as well as the hypothesis you may be working on for your research assignment. If your sources do not support your thesis, then you must adjust your thesis or track down additional sources and see if there is credible support for your ideas.

Examine Expertise of Author

What is the background of the author or authors? What are their credentials? Have they written other works on a similar subject? Do they have ties to industry or educational institutions or government agencies?

Look for Omissions

Think about what the author or agency chose to leave out of a particular document. Were important or significant issues left out? In a recent report by a government panel on dietary recommendations, little mention was made of reducing sugar intake. Further investigation revealed that a number of panel members had strong ties to the sugar lobby ("Food Pyramid" 2004). Sometimes reading magazine or newspaper articles about a document can provide useful information about the credibility of a report.

FIND STATISTICS

The U.S. government is the largest collector and publisher of statistical data in the world (Hernon, Dugan, Shuler 2003). Much of the work of data collection is scattered among almost seventy federal agencies, with the Bureau of the Census, the Bureau of Economic Analysis, and the Bureau of Labor Statistics collecting the largest amount of data (Robinson 1998).

Several compilations provide access to a great deal of data that the government collects. *Statistical Abstracts of the United States* and the commercial database *LexisNexis Statistical*, available in some libraries, provide answers to many statistical research needs. In addition, many free government web sites, such as FedStats, provide links to agency-collected statistical data. Though government statistics are viewed as highly reliable, the decentralized aspect of statistical gathering by the U.S. government does not always ensure that the data is accurate and without bias.

Use *Statistical Abstracts* to Locate Statistics

Statistical information about the United States, as well as more limited information about other countries, is compiled into one source—*Statistical Abstracts of the United States.* Available online (http://www.census.gov/statab/www/) and in print in most libraries, this resource summarizes statistical data from thousands of government and business sources. The summarized data is often sufficient, but information about the resource from which the data was abstracted is also provided. Most of the earlier editions of this publication are now available online, starting with the first, published in 1878.

Use Statistical Databases to Locate Statistics

Many statistical research needs can be met by using a variety of databases. These "meta-sites" pull together or provide links to many different types of statistics. Sometimes it is necessary to go a step further if the statistics needed are not available using the tools listed below. Going directly to a specific government agency that produces the type of statistics sought can be useful for getting the most up-to-date numbers.

- *LexisNexis Statistical*, available in some academic libraries, indexes and provides links to statistics from the federal government, international intergovernmental organizations like the United Nations, and private organizations.
- *FedStats* (http://www.fedstats.gov) is the best free site for statistics produced by about seventy federal agencies.
- The Census Bureau (http://www.census.gov) surveys the population every ten years by taking the Decennial Census. The Census includes information about people and housing. The Census web site has so much information that it can be difficult to navigate. Go directly to *American Factfinder* from the Census home page for information on the 1990 and 2000 census.
- *The County and City Databook* provides statistics on counties and cities. The current version is available online (http://www.census.gov/statab/www/ccdb.html), older print editions are in many libraries, and a few older editions are available online through the University of Virginia Libraries (http://fisher.lib.virginia.edu/collections/stats/ccdb/).
- The University of Michigan Documents Center (http://www.lib.umich.edu/govdocs/stats.html) provides a large collection of links to statistical resources on the web arranged by subject. This is a good tool for both U.S. and international statistics.
- The Social Statistics Briefing Room (http://www.whitehouse.gov/fsbr/ssbr.html) provides easy access to current statistics, including demographic, crime, health, and education statistics.

Find Historical Statistics

Older statistics can be found in earlier editions of *Statistical Abstracts* (http://www.census.gov/statab/www/) or by using *Historical Statistics of the United States, Colonial Times to 1970.* This two-volume collection of historical data supplements data found in the earlier editions of *Statistical Abstracts.* The Historical Census Browser at the University of Virginia Libraries (fisher.lib.virginia.edu/census) provides summary census data from 1790 to 1960. Older statistics can also be found by searching the library online catalog, mentioned below.

Use Secondary Sources to Locate Difficult-to-Find Statistics

Rather than reinventing the wheel by searching government web sites and publications to locate difficult-to-find statistics, it can be useful to "piggyback" on the work of other researchers. There is a high probability that some researcher before you also needed, for example, the infant mortality rate in Paraguay. Use chapter 3 of this book to determine the best journal article database for the topic under investigation. Use keywords, combined with the word "statistics" or other relevant terms, to search the topic. For example, in a specialized history journal index such as *America: History and Life*, the following search would turn up articles by researchers who had already collected data on a topic:

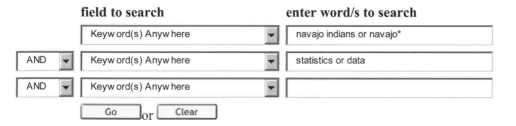

The "*" retrieves different endings (in this case "Navajos").

In some cases the list of references at the end of the article will lead you to the relevant statistical sources that were used by the author; in other cases the authors themselves will have done primary research and collected their own data.

Similarly, using the online catalog to find books that cover statistics on a given topic can be easier than tracking down the statistical sources from scratch. For example:

field to search		enter word/s to search
Keyw ord(s) Anyw here ▼		cambodia
AND ▼	Keyw ord(s) Anyw here ▼	statistics or data
AND ▼	Keyw ord(s) Anyw here ▼	

Go or Clear

CRITICALLY EVALUATE STATISTICS

The U.S. government is viewed as a reliable source for statistical information, but at the same time the process of gathering statistics is always subject to possible flaws or bias. Many constituencies have criticized the Decennial Census since its inception in 1790. Prior to 1840, U.S. Marshals relied on heads of households to report information about the inhabitants of their houses rather than doing a direct count. In 1840 reports on the number of blacks in the north classified as insane was extremely high. Northerners charged that southerners had corrupted the data in order to show that blacks were unsuited to freedom. Reforms were then made in the way data was collected and data collection has continued to be adjusted to the present day (Anderson 1988). Current criticisms include charges that certain populations, such as the homeless, have been systematically undercounted. Though Census statistics and other government-collected statistics are not without flaws, researchers continue to rely on these data because they are often the most accurate numbers available.

When using data for any research project, the following questions should be asked:

- Who collected the data? Was it an agency, a person, or a group? If it was an organization, does this organization have a particular agenda? Or was it an academic research institute that might have less bias and be less agenda-driven?
- Who analyzed the data? Was it the same organization that created the data, or was it an organization that took government data and did its own analysis? Does the group that did the analysis have a specific agenda, or is the group simply trying to further knowledge on a particular subject?
- How was the data actually collected? What process was used? Was it a systematic or random sample, or did it depend on volunteers to step forward and provide information? The method of data collection can have a huge impact on the degree to which the data can be generalized. Sometimes data collection techniques are explained in the notes section of an article or book.
- How current is the data? What date range does it include and when was it collected? This will differ from the date that the data was published.

- Is the data relevant to the research you are doing? This sounds like an obvious question, but it is important not to try to squeeze data into a research project when the data are not relevant to the subject under study.

Government documents and statistical resources provide rich content for research in many disciplines. Reports and data issued from the government tend to be more trusted than information issued by private organizations, though any individual resource could suffer from bias or poor research design. Information issued by the government is more widely available over the internet at no cost because it is exempt from copyright regulations. However, some of the more useful databases that provide access to these resources are only available by subscription through academic libraries and other organizations.

NOTE

1. On May 1, 2003, the White House's Office of the Press Secretary produced a press release which read, "President Bush Announces Combat Operations in Iraq Have Ended." Several months later, when the war was clearly still going strong, the White House went back and inserted the word "Major" before the word "Combat." The State Department and other web sites such as www.thememoryhole.org have copies of the original web page that was "depublished" by the White House.

REFERENCES

Ames, John Griffith. 1905. *Comprehensive index to the publications of the United States government, 1881–1893.* 2d ed. (58/2:H.doc. 754 [Serial set 4745 [v.I]; 4746 Iv.2]). Washington, DC: Government Printing Office.

Anderson, Margo. 1988. *The American Census: A social history.* New Haven, CT: Yale University Press.

Becker, Elizabeth. 2004. Kissinger tapes describe crises, war and stark photos of abuse. *New York Times,* Section A, Column 2 (27 May): 1.

The food pyramid scheme. 2004. *New York Times* editorial. Section A, Column 1 (1 September): 18.

Hernon, Peter, Harold Relyea, Robert Dugan, and Joan Cheverie. 2002. *United States government information: Policies and sources.* Westport, CT: Libraries Unlimited, 41.

Hernon, Peter, Robert Dugan, and John Shuler. 2003. *U.S. government on the web.* Westport, CT: Libraries Unlimited.

Johnson, Nancy. 1979. *Sources of compiled legislative histories: A bibliography of government documents, periodical articles, and books.* Littleton, CO: F.B. Rothman.

Lord, Clifford, ed. 1944. *Presidential Executive Orders.* New York: Archives Publishing.

Matthews, Mark. 2004. U.S. practices at Abu Ghraib barred in '80s; Interrogators now taught psychological methods. *Baltimore Sun* (11 May): 1a.

Milbank, Dana, and Mike Allen. 2003. Release of documents is delayed; Classified papers to be reviewed. *Washington Post* (26 March): A15.

National Council for Research on Women. 2004. *Missing: Information about women's lives,* March. http://www.ncrw.org/misinfo/report.htm. Accessed March 5, 2005.

Poore, Benjamin Perley, comp. 1885. *A descriptive catalogue of the government publications of the United States, September 5, 1774–March 4, 1881.* (48/2:S.misc.doc. 67 [Serial set 2268]). Washington, DC: Government Printing Office.

Pope, Carl. 2004. Whitewash at Ground Zero. *Sierra* 89, no. 1 (January/February): 8.

Robinson, Judith Schiek. 1998. *Tapping the government grapevine: The user-friendly guide to U.S. government information sources.* Phoenix, AZ: Oryx Press.

Union of Concerned Scientists. 2004. *Scientific integrity in policymaking: An investigation into the Bush administration misuse of science,* March. http://www.ucsusa.org/global_environment/rsi/page.cfm?pageID=1641. Accessed March 3, 2005.

U.S. Congress, Senate. 1913. *The mission of woman.* By Albert Taylor Bledsoe. S. Doc. 174, 63rd Cong., 1st sess., Serial 6537.

8

Citing Sources, Avoiding Plagiarism, and Organizing References

Copy from one, it's plagiarism; copy from two, it's research.
Wilson Mizner

Scholarly research is an ongoing conversation among scholars that takes place in journals, books, reports, and conference proceedings. No research is done in a vacuum. Scholars present their research in the context of other studies that have been conducted. They use past research as a building block for their own investigations. The Mizner quote above suggests that research in some sense is like an act of plagiarism, because in any scholarly work a certain portion is dedicated to summarizing what others have discovered about a topic. What separates scholarship from *being* plagiarism is that any information that is the product of someone else's research is carefully cited in a bibliography or list of references. Failure to cite another person's intellectual production is considered theft.

When you write a research paper you are entering the scholarly conversation. By acknowledging the work that has taken place prior to your research, you are placing your own ideas within the context of what is already known about a subject. Citing other sources demonstrates that you are engaged with the research that has gone on before you and honors the creators of the intellectual property upon which your work is based. Citing other scholars strengthens your research by showing that your arguments are supported by other scholars and also that you are aware of research some scholars have put forward that disagrees with your analysis. Scholarship is an act of collaboration. By writing a research paper, you are becoming a part of this group effort in discovery. Your participation requires the acknowledgement of important ideas upon which your own are based.

By acknowledging the sources you have used to construct your own research, you avoid committing plagiarism. Plagiarism can be accidental or planned, but, as the following cases illustrate, the results are often the same.

In 2002 it was discovered that Pulitzer Prize winner Doris Kearns Goodwin had failed to cite some of her sources in her book *The Fitzgeralds and the Kennedys*. She confessed that note-taking for the book had been sloppy and that the failure to cite sources was unintentional. The press and her fellow scholars deemed it plagiarism. Since the incident, invitations to speaking engagements have been withdrawn, her resignation was accepted for her seat on the Pulitzer board, and she has taken leave from her role as a commentator on *The News Hour with Jim Lehrer* on PBS.

Jayson Blair, a young star reporter for the *New York Times* was found to have systematically fabricated and plagiarized news stories for years. Blair and two top editors at the *New York Times* were dismissed. Blair's career as a serious journalist was over.

Senator Joseph Biden was forced to drop out of the 1997 Democratic presidential primary due to the discovery that he was not only plagiarizing passages of other politicians' speeches, but he had flunked a course in law school twenty years earlier after plagiarizing a legal article. Biden claimed he was unaware that legal briefs required the acknowledgement of sources, but damage to his reputation was significant.

This chapter provides information on how to develop a system for taking notes, when to paraphrase or use direct quotations, how to properly cite a source, how to use specialized software to format your footnotes or endnotes, and how to bring critical evaluation techniques into the process.

DEVELOP A SYSTEM FOR TAKING NOTES

Accidental copying and plagiarism can often begin at the note-taking stage of research. There are many different techniques available for taking notes. Start with a consistent plan of how to collect information and stick to it. Because so many resources are now online, much of your note-taking will take place online using cut and paste techniques. It is important to be selective in what you choose to retain in your collection of notes. It is all too easy to become inundated with hundreds of pages of notes. Consider cutting and pasting and then weeding out what is not important, or select only specific paragraphs to cut and paste from what you have read. Whatever system you devise, the following tactics should be employed:

- As you cut and paste information from a source, *always* copy the full citation—author, title, date, and publishing information—at the same time. If citing a web page, note the date that you viewed the page. Though time-consuming, this process will save you an enormous amount of time at the end stage of your research.
- Either put all your notes in a separate Word document or change the font color of any text that is not your own so that you will not mix up your own words with that of another author when you are writing your paper.
- Use bold or brackets to indicate any comments or paraphrases that are in your own words rather than that of the source document. It is useful to try to summarize or put into your own words the gist of the content you may end up using in your research. This helps you digest or integrate the information into your own internal knowledge bank and will be helpful to use later when you incorporate ideas into your research paper.
- Incorporate any handwritten notes into your electronic collection of notes.

Paraphrase or Summarize Carefully

Resist the temptation to fill your paper with direct quotations from other authors. Most of your references to the research that has preceded yours should be in the form of a summary or paraphrase. A *summary* is a concise overview of another author's ideas and should be used whenever possible. For example:

Original Authors' Words:
Today's Net Gen college students have grown up with technology. Born around the time the PC was introduced, 20 percent began using computers between the ages of 5 and 8. Virtually all Net Gen students were using computers by the time they were 16 to 18 years of age. Computer usage is even higher among today's children. Among children ages 8 to 18, 96 percent have gone online. Seventy-four percent have access at home, and 61 percent use the Internet on a typical day. (Oblinger and Oblinger 2005)

Summary:
Most of today's college students began using computers at a young age, and the majority of these students log onto the internet on any given day (Oblinger and Oblinger 2005).

A *paraphrase* restates the author's words, usually in about the same number of words as the original publication.

Original Authors' Words:

When teenagers were asked what they want from the Internet, the most common response is to get "new information." Close behind, at about 75 percent, is to "learn more or to learn better." (Oblinger and Oblinger 2005)

Paraphrase:

Teenagers reported that the most common reason they log onto the internet is to get information. The next most common reason is to learn more. (Oblinger and Oblinger 2005)

There are times, however, when the author has already stated an idea concisely and powerfully and you will want to use that author's precise words by quoting from him or her directly.

Direct Quotation:

The goal of relinking work and family life is not simple. . . . It is about shifting to a more equitable society in which family and community are valued as much as paid work is valued and where men and women have equal opportunity to achieve in both spheres. (Rapaport and Bailyn 1996, 28)

When you paraphrase text, you are putting the text into your own words. By using summaries and paraphrases in your work, you are demonstrating that you understand the work you are using and are integrating other scholars' ideas and research into your own work. Using the work of other scholars places your work in the larger research picture and provides validity for the ideas you are putting forward. Paraphrasing is a difficult but important skill to attain—it involves forcing yourself to actively digest what you are reading.

Always cite your source when you paraphrase or summarize an idea that is not your own, unless it is common knowledge. Many facts are so well established and commonly known that it is not necessary to provide a citation. The dates that the United States was involved in World War II, for example, are well established. Other ideas, such as the reasons the United States entered World War II, are less well established and need to be backed up by citations. When in doubt, cite your source. It is not overkill to have a citation in every other paragraph of a research paper.

When you are paraphrasing or summarizing be careful not to borrow too much of the original author's language. If you cannot avoid this, use a direct quotation instead. Also, be careful to provide an accurate paraphrase of the author's original work. Do not bend someone's words to fit your own research agenda.

Limit Use of Direct Quotations

Use quotations when the original words are especially powerful, eloquent, or cannot be easily paraphrased. A direct quotation involves putting down another author's words exactly as they appear. If the words consist of less than a few lines, you can incorporate them into the text of your paper by using quotation marks to set them apart from your own words. If the words consist of more than three to four lines of text, set them as a block quotation—double indent five spaces from the left-hand margin and five spaces from the right-hand margin and set the quotation apart with an extra line space before and after the quotation. Quotation marks are not needed when the quotation is indented. The sentence that precedes the quotation should set the stage for the quotation; the sentence following it should be used as a transition back to your own writing.

When you use direct quotations, use ellipses (three dots in the middle of a sentence and four at the end of a sentence) to leave out information that is not relevant to the point you are making, but do not change the original intent of the text. When necessary, use brackets to insert your own words in order to clarify the meaning of a quotation taken out of context. For example: "He [Tony Blair] was waiting for an important call."

Whenever possible avoid direct quotations and use paraphrasing and summarizing instead. These techniques allow you to do a better job of integrating the work with your own research.

Avoid Overuse of Citations

You can have too many citations in your paper if you cite information that is already commonly known or if you spend most of your research paper reporting the research of others rather than putting forward some of your own ideas and analysis.

In the following example neither citation is needed because these facts about the Industrial Revolution are widely agreed upon and commonly known.

The Industrial Revolution completely transformed the meaning of work in American life (Smith 2001). With the advent of factories, work became completely severed from the home, many jobs involved routine and monotonous tasks, and new roles developed within the workplace between managers and workers. (Lopez 2003)

In the next two examples, citations are needed—the first for a statistic that was found in a particular source, the second because it involves one author's theory about the goals of industrialists.

In 1860, 60 percent of the labor force were engaged in farming (U.S. Bureau of the Census 1976).

With the rise of capitalism and the growing importance of the workplace as a primary institution in society, industrialists sought to place work at the center of life and incorporate families more completely into serving the needs of the organization (Kanter 1977).

STEER CLEAR OF ALL TYPES OF PLAGIARISM

Plagiarism, from a Latin word meaning "kidnapping," ranges from inept paraphrasing to outright theft.
Harry Shaw, *Concise Dictionary of Literary Terms* (1975)

Plagiarism means copying the ideas or language of another writer without formally acknowledging that writer. It is intellectual theft and it is treated severely at most schools. There are many different types of plagiarism.

- Direct plagiarism consists of taking the exact words of an author and copying them into your own paper without citing the author.
- Indirect plagiarism occurs when a paraphrase is too close to the original words of the author. In this case providing a citation does not exempt you from the offense—if the paraphrase is too close to the words in the original, you must quote directly and indent the words or use quotation marks to demonstrate that it is an exact quote.
- Accidental plagiarism occurs when the writer simply forgets to cite a source due to sloppiness or poor note-taking procedures. Unintentional plagiarism is punished just as harshly as direct plagiarism.
- Another form of direct plagiarism consists of buying a paper from a friend or term paper mill and signing your name to it. This is one of the most serious types of plagiarism and one of the easiest to spot. You are equally culpable if you sell or give one of your papers to a friend to pass off as his or her own.

Today, with so many resources online, it is easy to conduct most of your note-taking online. By cutting and pasting material for your research paper, it can be easy to confuse a scholar's work with your own. It can also be tempting to cut and paste portions of your notes into your research paper without attributing these ideas to their original author. Any type of plagiarism, whether accidental or intentional, is treated seriously in academic settings. Many schools require instructors to give students failing grades or, in some cases, suspend students for representing another writer's work and ideas as their own.

The same technology that facilitates copying also facilitates the discovery of copying. Most universities now subscribe to plagiarism software that provides faculty members with simple tools that enable them to detect plagiarism. In addition, many teachers are able to detect plagiarism in their own field because they are familiar with the works of important scholars in their area of research. The easiest way to avoid plagiarism is to *cite any sources you use for your research*, unless what you are writing about is a commonly accepted fact such as the temperature at which water will freeze or the date that Bill Clinton became president.

CHOOSE A STYLE MANUAL

A style manual is a book that indicates exactly how to format the citations that are listed in the references section at the end of a research paper or published work. Style manuals also provide information about many aspects of writing a research paper. Some instructors prefer a particular style manual, but many instructors will be content if you use one of the major style manuals available and use it consistently. The three most frequently used style manuals are listed below.

The Chicago Manual of Style. 15th ed. Chicago: University of Chicago Press, 2003.
A Manual for Writers of Term Papers, Theses, and Dissertations. 6th ed. Edited by Kate L. Turabian, John Grossman, and Alice Bennett. Chicago: University of Chicago Press, 1996.
MLA Style Manual and Guide to Scholarly Publishing. 2nd ed. Edited by Joseph Gibaldi. New York: Modern Language Association of America, 1998.

In addition, there are discipline-specific style manuals that are sometimes used.

Biology

Scientific Style and Format: The CBE Manual for Authors, Editors, and Publishers. 6th ed. Cambridge: Cambridge University Press, 1994.

Chemistry

The ACS Style Guide: A Manual for Authors and Editors. 2nd ed. Edited by Janet S. Dodd. Washington, DC: American Chemical Society, 1997.

Law

The Blue Book: A Uniform System of Citation. 17th ed. Cambridge, MA: Harvard Law Review Association, 2000.

Medicine

National Library of Medicine Recommended Formats for Bibliographic Citation. Edited by Karen Patrias. Bethesda, MD: U.S. Dept. of Health and Human Services, Public Health Service, National Institutes of Health, National Library of Medicine, Reference Section, 1991. A supplement to this guide covering internet formats is available online at http://www.nlm.nih.gov/pubs/formats/internet.pdf.

Psychology

Publication Manual of the American Psychological Association. 5th ed. Washington, DC: American Psychological Association, 2001. (APA's web site provides information on how to cite electronic documents.)

Sociology

ASA Style Guide. 2nd ed. Washington, DC: American Sociological Association, 1997.

CHOOSE A DOCUMENTATION STYLE

Once you choose a style manual, you need to decide whether to use abbreviated citations, placed within parentheses in the text of your paper, or sequentially numbered footnotes that correlate to citations at the bottom of each page or to endnotes at the end of your research paper. Each discipline (e.g., psychology, chemistry), uses a specific style of documentation best suited to the needs of that discipline.

Humanities scholars, historians, and legal studies scholars use footnotes or endnotes instead of parenthetical citations placed within the text. Footnotes and endnotes are raised Arabic numerals that follow the punctuation mark. For example: *Some researchers have found that increased regulation of gun ownership results in fewer deaths.*[1] The numbered notes are then listed at the bottom of the relevant page (footnote), or at the end of a paper (endnote), followed by a citation to the text being referenced.

Social scientists and scientists use parenthetical citations with an author and date, for example: (Lopez 1999). In addition, social scientists use parenthetical citations with author, date, *and* page number when referring to a particular point made in the text (Lopez 1999, 23). When an abbreviated parenthetical citation has been made within the text, a complete citation indicating the author, title, date, and publication information is placed at the end of the paper. This list of citations is titled "References" or "Bibliography" or "Works Cited." In some cases a bibliography might list additional works that have been read but not necessarily directly cited within the text. These references are listed alphabetically. In addition to parenthetical footnotes, numbered notes are sometimes used sparingly to convey information that is tangential to the purpose of the text.

If you are not sure how to document your citations, find a journal that is in the same discipline as the course for which you are writing a paper. Look at an article in that journal and notice if the abbreviated citations are surrounded by parentheses and placed within the text, or if numbered footnotes are used. Another option is to ask your instructor what documentation format to use for your paper.

USE THE FOLLOWING EXAMPLES FROM THE *CHICAGO MANUAL OF STYLE* TO FORMAT YOUR REFERENCES

At the end of your paper, each source you have cited will be listed either alphabetically or in the order mentioned in your paper. Once you have determined which style manual you need to use, consult that manual in order to use the appropriate formatting for your references.

The following are examples from the *Chicago Manual of Style*, the most commonly used style manual, indicating exactly where to place your author, title, and publishing information. These examples are the most frequently cited types of works. For further examples and more complex citations, consult the *Chicago Manual of Style*, using the index located in the back of the book, or use a style manual recommended by your instructor. The *Chicago Manual of Style* can be found at any research or public library. The purpose of a citation is to provide your reader with enough information to be able to find the source you are citing.

Citing Different Types of Books

A citation to a book must include the following:

- name of author(s) or editor(s),
- title,
- place of publication and publisher,
- date published.

Additional information could include the edition, if not the first; volume, if more than one; series title, if applicable; and a URL, if located on the web (along with the name of the ebook collection, if it exists), or other information about the medium (such as CD-ROM format).

Single Author

Rogers, Mary F. *Barbie Culture.* Thousand Oaks, CA: Sage, 1999.

Multi-Author

Back, Les, Tim Crabbe, and John Solomos. *The Changing Face of Football: Racism, Identity and Multiculture in the English Game.* Oxford: New York: Berg, 2001.

Edited Volume

Combs, James, ed. *Movies and Politics: The Dynamic Relationship.* New York: Garland, 1993.

Article or Chapter within an Edited Book

Hameed, Shahul. "India and China: The Economic Relationship." In *The Peacock and the Dragon: India-China Relations in the 21st Century*, edited by Kanti Bajpai and Amitabh Mattoo. New Delhi: Har-Anand Publications, 2000.

Ebook

Giele, Janet Z., and Leslie F. Stebbins. *Women and Equality in the Workplace: A Reference Handbook.* Santa Barbara, CA: 2003. Available on *NetLibrary*, http://www.netlibrary.com (accessed July 14, 2004).

Citing Articles in Journals, Newspapers, or Magazines

Citations to articles include the following:

- author name(s),
- title of article,
- name of journal, newspaper, or magazine in which the article appeared,
- volume number, issue number (if one exists), date published, and page reference (if appropriate).

Page numbers for newspaper and magazine articles can be omitted, but you should cite the edition and section of a newspaper if they are available. Online articles are cited in the same way, with the addition of a URL web address followed by the date the article was viewed. If the article was viewed as part of a database collection of journals accessed through a library, see the appropriate example below for additional information.

Scholarly Journal Article

Fisher, Nick. "The Physics of Your Pint: Head of Beer Exhibits Exponential Decay." *Physics Education* 39 (2004): 34–36.

Newspaper Article

Corrigan, Maureen. "The Trials of Juggling a Baby and Briefcase." *New York Times*, 8 May 2002, sec. E, late edition.

Magazine Article

N'Gai, Croal. "He's Got Games." *Newsweek*, 29 December 2003, 101–102.

Online Journal Article

Legg, Stephen. "Gendered Politics and Nationalised Homes: Women and the Anti-Colonial Struggle in Delhi." *Gender Place and Culture: A Journal of Feminist Geography* 10, no. 1 (March 2003), http://www.tandf.co.uk/journals/carfax/0966369X.html (accessed January 5, 2004).

Online Journal from a Database

Waller, John C. "Becoming a Darwinian: The Micro-politics of Sir Francis Galton's Scientific Career." *Annals of Science* (2004): 141–164. In EBSCO [online database]. Cited January 4, 2004. Available from Brandeis University Libraries.

Citing a Stand Alone Web Page

The date a web page is viewed is an essential component in a citation for a "stand alone" web page, or home page, that is not an issue of a magazine, journal, or other regular publication. The citation should include the author or (if the author's name is not available) the organization, the title, the URL, and the date viewed. If you have reason to suspect that the web page is of a very temporary nature, you may want to look for another source from which to cite your information.

Food and Drug Administration. *Tattoos, Temporary Tattoos and Henna Products.* Available at http://www.fda.gov/oc/opacom/hottopics/tattoos.html (accessed October 11, 2004).

For any information sources—such as conference proceedings or government documents—that fall outside of the more frequently cited categories mentioned above, consult the full edition of the *Chicago Manual of Style* or another style manual.

USE BIBLIOGRAPHIC SOFTWARE TO CITE YOUR SOURCES

Bibliographic software programs provide the researcher with a personalized inventory, in database form, of citations and other information on books, articles, documents, web pages, and other resources. For short papers the "Footnotes" option located in Microsoft Word or other word processing programs will suffice. For longer papers it is useful to create a database of citations that can be called up at any time and inserted into a research paper in a variety of different formats. These software programs allow the researcher to "cite while you write" by automatically inserting citations into a paper in whatever citation style is preferred (i.e., *Chicago Manual of Style* or *MLA*). These programs are also designed to work with library online catalogs and journal databases so that while the tools are being used, you can import records directly into your citation software and have them at your disposal when writing your paper.

The four major bibliographic software options are Procite, Endnote, Reference Manager, and Refworks. Of the four, Refworks is the only one that is internet based. All four provide the basic capabilities needed for keeping track of your references and also provide you with the ability to:

- save a record of each resource into a personal database;
- organize, search, and retrieve records by categories, such as "author" or "subject";
- integrate with word processing to insert footnotes or endnotes;
- format citations according to all the major style manuals.

Choosing which tool to use rests on which bells and whistles you prefer, which package your college or university supports, and personal preferences about the software interface. There are also a number of less sophisticated programs, such as EasyBib.com, available for free online.

BRING EVALUATION INTO THE PROCESS

Research involves diving into an ongoing scholarly conversation. Every journal article you read and decide to include in your note-taking, every resource you choose to cite in your paper, has undergone a vetting process initiated by you. Interspersed with everything you include in your research are all the articles, books, and other sources of information that you have chosen to ignore—either purposefully because they did not warrant inclusion, or neglectfully because you did not do a comprehensive review of the literature on your topic or put a conscious effort into your review process. Ultimately, your research can only be as good as the references that surround it.

At the start of a research project, it is difficult to select the most important information to include in your notes. Initially it is wise to include more than you might need because information that may seem off topic at first may come to be useful later. As your hypothesis becomes more focused over time and as you read more on a subject, it will be easier to spot information that is relevant to your topic and that is new and valid.

REFERENCES

Kanter, Rosabeth Moss. 1977. *Work and family in the United States: A critical review and agenda for research and policy.* New York: Russell Sage Foundation.

Oblinger, Diana G., and James L. Oblinger, eds. 2005. *Educating the net generation.* Boulder, CO: Educause. Ebook available at www.educause.edu/educatingthenetgen/.

Rapaport, Rhona, and Lotte Bailyn. 1996. *Relinking life and work: Toward a better future. A report to the Ford Foundation based on a collaborative research project with three corporations.* New York: Ford Foundation.

Shaw, Harry. 1975. *Concise dictionary of literary terms.* New York: McGraw-Hill.

U.S. Bureau of the Census. 1976. *Historical statistics of the United States, colonial times to 1970.* Washington, DC: Government Printing Office.

Appendix: Specialized Journal Article Databases: Indexes and Full Text

Specialized article databases provide citations and in some cases the full text of articles in journals from a specific discipline or subject area (such as psychology or anthropology). Choose the discipline in which you are working from the alphabetical list below. Then log onto your library web page and look under "databases" or "electronic resources" to see if your library owns the relevant databases.

African and African American Studies

This is an interdisciplinary field. See other disciplines such as sociology, literature, or history to choose additional databases.

African Studies Indexes journal articles and other resources related to the study of Africa.

Ethnic NewsWatch Indexing and full text of hundreds of newspapers, magazines, and journals of the American ethnic press.

Agriculture

AGRICOLA Indexes journal articles and other resources in agriculture and related fields.

ASAE Technical Library American Society of Agricultural Engineers (ASAE) standards, journals, and conference proceedings.

CAB Abstracts Indexes journals and other sources from the agricultural literature throughout the world.

American Studies

This is an interdisciplinary field. See other disciplines such as literature or anthropology to choose additional databases.

America: History and Life Indexes journals, books, and dissertations on U.S. and Canadian history and culture.

Ethnic NewsWatch Indexing and full text of hundreds of newspapers, magazines, and journals of the American ethnic press.

Sociological Abstracts Indexes and abstracts journal articles and books in sociology, social work, and other social sciences.

Anthropology

Anthropological Index Online Indexes journal literature held in the Anthropology Library at the British Museum.

Anthropology Plus Indexes articles on all anthropological topics.

Applied Science and Technology

Applied Science and Technology Index Indexes hundreds of scientific and technical publications.

Compendex Indexes thousands of journals in engineering and related technical fields.

INSPEC Indexes thousands of scholarly journals and other resources in physics, electrical engineering and electronics, computers and control, and information technology.

Archaelogy

Anthropology Plus Indexes articles on all anthropological topics.

L'Annee Philologique Indexes over two thousand books, journals, dissertations, conference papers, and collections covering all aspects of Greco-Roman antiquity.

Asian and Asian American Studies

This is an interdisciplinary field. See other disciplines such as sociology, literature, or history to choose additional databases.

Bibliography of Asian Studies Indexes thousands of journal articles, books, and conference proceedings worldwide on the countries, histories, and cultures of East, South, and Southeast Asia.

Ethnic NewsWatch   Indexes over two hundred ethnic, minority, and native press publications. Contains news, culture, and history.

Art, Architecture, and Photography

Art Full Text   Indexes hundreds of international publications, including journals, yearbooks, museum bulletins, film reviews, bibliographies, conference reports, review articles, interviews, and exhibition listings.

Art Index and Art Index Retrospective   Indexes more than 250 journals in the visual arts, as well as other resources in the arts such as exhibition catalogs.

Avery Index to Architectural Periodicals   Indexes scholarly and professional journals covering architecture and related fields. Many titles go back to the 1930s.

Bibliography of the History of Art   Indexes and abstracts journals, books, exhibition catalogs, and other materials in the arts.

Biochemistry

BIOSIS Previews   Indexes thousands of international journals in the life sciences.

PubMed   Indexes thousands of biomedical journals.

SciFinder Scholar   Indexes the world's literature in chemistry, biochemistry, and related fields.

Bioengineering

PubMed   Indexes journal literature in the fields of medicine and life sciences.

Biology

BIOSIS Previews   Indexes thousands of international journals in the life sciences.

PubMed   Indexes thousands of biomedical journals.

SciFinder Scholar   Indexes the world's literature in chemistry and related fields.

Business

ABI/Inform Global   Index and some full text to more than a thousand scholarly, popular, and trade periodicals related to business, management, finance, and economics.

Business Source Premier Full text and indexing to thousands of journals in business.

LexisNexis Academic Full-text news, business, industry, and legal information.

Regional Business News Full text of business journals, newspapers, and newswires from all metropolitan and rural areas within the United States.

Chemistry

arXive Free access to preprints for physics, chemistry, mathematics, computer science, and quantitative biology.

SciFinder Scholar Indexes the world's literature in chemistry and related fields.

Classical and Medieval Studies

DYABOLA An index to one of the world's largest and oldest collections of books, journals, and research material on classical, Egyptian, and Near Eastern archaeology and ancient history.

International Medieval Bibliography Indexes thousands of journals and other resources covering all aspects of the middle ages.

ITER: Gateway to the Renaissance Indexes hundreds of journal titles on the Middle Ages and the Renaissance.

L'Année Philologique Indexes publications covering all aspects of Greco-Roman antiquity.

Computer Science

ACM Digital Library Indexing and full text for articles published in Association for Computing Machinery periodicals and proceedings and other sources.

arXive Preprints for physics, mathematics, nonlinear sciences, computer science, and quantitative biology.

Economics

EconLit Indexes journals, books, dissertations, and working papers in economics.

PAIS (Public Affairs Information Service) Indexes over one thousand journals, books, and government documents on public policy aspects of business, economics, government, and other social science topics.

Education

Education Index and Education Full Text Indexing and full text to journals in education.

ERIC Indexes journal articles and other educational resources.

Engineering

Compendex Indexes thousands of journals in engineering and related technical fields.

IEEE Xplore Indexes Institute of Electrical and Electronics Engineers transactions, journals, magazines, and conference proceedings.

INSPEC Indexes thousands of scholarly journals and other resources in physics, electrical engineering and electronics, computers and control, and information technology.

Environmental Studies

This is an interdisciplinary field. See other disciplines such as sociology, literature, or politics to choose additional databases.

BIOSIS Previews Indexes thousands of international journals in the life sciences.

Environmental Sciences and Pollution Management Indexes thousands of journals and other materials related to the environmental sciences.

PubMed Indexes thousands of biomedical journals.

SciFinder Scholar Indexes the world's literature in chemistry and related fields.

Wildlife and Ecology Studies Worldwide Indexes literature on wild mammals, birds, reptiles, and amphibians.

European Cultural Studies

This is an interdisciplinary field. See other disciplines such as sociology, literature, or politics to choose additional databases.

Historical Abstracts Indexes journals, books, and dissertations on European and world history, not including the United States and Canada.

MLA Bibliography Indexes journals and other resources in literature, language, linguistics, and folklore.

Film Studies

Art Index Indexes articles and film reviews in more than 250 journals in the arts.

Film Index International   Indexes articles and other resources on all types of films from around the world.

Film Literature Index   Indexes articles and other resources on all types of films from around the world.

MLA Bibliography   Indexes journals and other resources in literature, language, linguistics, and folklore.

Readers' Guide Retrospective   Indexes and abstracts more than two hundred popular magazines published in the United States, from 1890 through 1982.

French Language and Literature

ARTFL   A French textual database with thousands of articles, including literary criticism and other fields.

MLA Bibliography   Indexes journals and other resources in literature, language, linguistics, and folklore.

German Studies

IBZ—Internationale Bibliographie der Zeitschriftenliteratur   Indexes thousands of journals worldwide, specializing in the humanities and the social sciences.

IDZ Index deutschsprachiger Zeitschriften   Indexes several hundred German-language journals, mostly in the humanities and social sciences.

MLA Bibliography   Indexes journals and other resources in literature, language, linguistics, and folklore.

Health and Medicine

CINAHL   Indexes journal literature related to nursing and allied health.

Medline and PubMed   The National Library of Medicine database. Covers thousands of journal titles and is international in scope.

History

America: History and Life   Indexes journals, books, and dissertations on U.S. and Canadian history and culture.

Historical Abstracts   Indexes journals, books, and dissertations on European and world history, not including the United States and Canada.

Nineteenth Century Masterfile   Indexes periodicals, books, newspapers, and government documents from the nineteenth century.

Italian Language and Literature

MLA Bibliography Indexes journals and other resources in literature, language, linguistics, and folklore.

Journalism and Media Studies

LexisNexis Academic Full text of U.S. newspapers and some newspapers from other countries.

Newspaper Abstracts Index and summaries of dozens of newspapers from the United States.

PAIS (Public Affairs Information Service) Indexes over one thousand journals, books, and government documents on public policy aspects of business, economics, government, and other social science topics.

Latin American Studies

Ethnic NewsWatch Indexing and full text of hundreds of newspapers, magazines, and journals of the American ethnic press.

Handbook of Latin American Studies Online Selective listing of scholarly works on Latin America in the humanities and social sciences, including journal articles.

Hispanic American Periodicals Index (HAPI) Indexes articles on Central and South America, Mexico, the Caribbean, and Hispanics in the United States.

Legal Studies

Hein Online Provides full text to the early issues of many legal journals and law reviews, as well as other law journals and documents.

Index to Foreign Legal Periodicals Indexes articles from hundreds of legal periodicals and other resources on public and private international law.

LegalTrac Indexes journals, law reviews, and magazines related to legal research.

LexisNexis Academic—Law Review File Contains full-text law reviews and journals.

Linguistics

Linguistics Abstracts Online Indexes over three hundred linguistics journals.

Linguistics and Language Behavior Abstracts Indexes journals and other resources relating to the study of language.

MLA Bibliography Indexes journals and other resources in literature, language, linguistics, and folklore.

PsycInfo Indexes journal literature in psychology and related fields.

Literature

Literature Resource Center Full text of biographies, bibliographies, and critical analysis of authors from every age and literary discipline.

MLA Bibliography Indexes journals and other resources in literature, language, linguistics, and folklore.

Mathematics

arXive Preprints for physics, mathematics, nonlinear sciences, computer science, and quantitative biology.

MathSciNet Indexes journals in mathematics.

Middle Eastern Studies

This is an interdisciplinary field. See other disciplines such as sociology, literature, or politics to choose additional databases.

Index Islamicus Indexes journals and other resources related to Islam, the Middle East, and the Muslim world.

Music

International Index to Music Periodicals Indexes hundreds of international music journals from over twenty countries.

Music Index Indexes hundreds of international music journals and magazines covering every aspect of the classical and popular world of music.

RILM Abstracts of Musical Literature Indexes journals and other resources in music.

RIPM Retrospective Index to Music Periodicals Historical index to music journals.

Native American Studies

This is an interdisciplinary field. See other disciplines such as sociology, literature, or history to choose additional databases.

America: History and Life Indexes journals, books, and dissertations on U.S. and Canadian history and culture.

Ethnic NewsWatch Indexing and full text of hundreds of newspapers, magazines, and journals of the American ethnic press.

Philosophy

Philosophers Index Indexes journals and some books covering scholarly research in philosophy.

Physical Education/Athletics

CINAHL Index to articles that cover the psychology and/or sociology of medicine and allied health fields.

General Science Abstracts Articles that cover all aspects of general science, including sports medicine.

Physics

arXive Preprints for physics, mathematics, nonlinear sciences, computer science, and quantitative biology.

INSPEC Indexes journals in physics and computer science.

SciFinder Scholar Indexes the world's literature in chemistry and related fields.

Politics

PAIS (Public Affairs Information Service) Indexes over one thousand journals, books, and government documents on public policy aspects of business, economics, government, and other social science topics.

CIAO (Columbia International Affairs Online) Indexes journals and other resources related to international affairs.

Social Sciences Abstracts Indexes and abstracts articles in hundreds of international English-language social science journals.

Worldwide Political Science Abstracts Indexes journals in political science and related fields.

Psychology and Cognitive Sciences

MIT CogNet Provides searchable electronic texts in cognitive and brain sciences.

PsycInfo and PsycARTICLES   Indexes journal literature and other resources in psychology.

Social Sciences Abstracts   Indexes and abstracts articles in hundreds of international English-language social science journals.

Public Policy

PAIS (Public Affairs Information Service)   Indexes over one thousand journals, books, and government documents on public policy aspects of business, economics, government, and other social science topics.

PolicyFile   Indexes and links to full text of policy reports and documents from a wide range of thinks tanks, nongovernmental organizations, and international governmental organizations.

Religious Studies

ATLA Religion Database   Indexes journal articles, books, and dissertations on all aspects of world religions.

RAMBI Web Catalog   Indexes scholarly articles on Jewish studies and Israel.

Slavic and East European Studies

This is an interdisciplinary field. See other disciplines such as sociology, literature, or politics to choose additional databases.

ABSEES Online Database   Indexes journal articles and other resources published in the United States and Canada on East and Central Europe, Russia, and the former Soviet Union.

Russian Academy of Sciences Bibliographies   Covers thousands of journals published primarily in Russia, the republics of the former Soviet Union, and countries in Eastern Europe.

Sociology

SocIndex   Indexes and provides some full-text articles to journals in sociology and related disciplines.

Social Sciences Abstracts   Indexes and abstracts articles in hundreds of international English-language social science journals.

Sociological Abstracts   Indexes and abstracts journal articles and books in sociology, social work, and other social science.

Theater and Dance

International Index to the Performing Arts   Indexes hundreds of scholarly and popular performing arts journals and other resources.

Literature Resource Center   Full text of biographies, bibliographies, and critical analysis of authors from every age and literary discipline.

MLA Bibliography   Indexes journals and other resources in literature, language, linguistics, and folklore.

New York Public Library Dance Collection Catalog   Indexes journals and other resources from around the world on dance and dance culture.

Women and Gender Studies

Contemporary Women's Issues   Indexes and provides full text to hundreds of journals, newsletters, and reports.

GenderWatch   Includes magazines, journals, and other materials that focus on the impact of gender across a broad spectrum of subject areas.

Sexual Diversity Studies   Indexes journals and other resources concerning the gay, lesbian, bisexual, and transgender community.

Women's Studies International   Indexes journal and other resources related to women's studies.

Glossary

abstract A brief summary of the content of an information resource that presents the main points of the work. In a scholarly journal article, the abstract precedes the text and provides a useful overview of the article.

aggregator A large, usually multidisciplinary, collection of full-text articles from various publishers.

almanac A compendium of facts, statistics, and dates. An almanac can be general (such as a world almanac) or related to a particular academic subject (such as women's studies).

archives Collections of documents and records from organizations, which can include the personal or work-related papers of those associated with an organization.

atlas A collection of maps usually related to a subject or theme.

authentication 1. A security procedure that researchers have to go through when they are using online resources belonging to a library from an off-campus computer. This process verifies that the researcher is affiliated with the institution or library. 2. An investigative process that determines if an object is what it claims to be, if it is genuine. This term is used in verifying materials from archives, special collections, and web pages.

authority The credentials of an author, publisher, or sponsor of an information resource. In an academic setting authors are frequently evaluated by their institutional affiliation, previously published works, and reviews of their works.

autobiography A nonfiction account of a person's life written by its subject.

bibliographic software A computer program that provides the researcher with a personalized inventory, in database form, of citations and other information on books, articles, and other resources. This software works in conjunction with word processing software.

bibliography   A list of books, articles, web sites, and other resources that have been collected in a book, web site, or journal article. A summary is usually provided for each title listed.

biography   A history of the life of an individual. Usually considered nonfiction.

blog   A web page that provides frequent short entries arranged in reverse chronological order about a specific topic or subject.

Boolean searching   A system, developed by mathematician George Boole, which allows the researcher to combine words or phrases when searching a library online catalog or other database. The three Boolean operators are "or" (used for capturing synonyms), "and" (used for combining concepts), and "not" (used to exclude specific words or phrases).

broadcast search.   *See* **federated search engine**

chronology   A reference book or portion of a reference book that lists events in the order in which they occurred. Most chronologies cover a particular historical period, event, or subject.

citation   A reference to a particular book, article, or other source of information that includes author, title, and publication date, at minimum.

controlled vocabulary   A preferred term that is used as a subject heading in a library catalog, database, or index. Controlled vocabulary words are carefully developed in an effort to reflect the most common word used for a topic. Searching a database using the proper subject headings or controlled vocabulary can result in more relevant search results.

creator bias   Every creator or author of an information resource has a point of view or bias that must be factored in when evaluating the information. Scholarly journals that go through a peer-review process are less prone to creator bias. Primary sources such as diaries can be strongly influenced by the views of their creator.

critical evaluation   Critical evaluation involves using analytical thinking skills within the context of conducting research. Critical evaluation is an active process that comes into play at every stage of the research process—during topic selection; choosing databases to search; selecting books, articles, and other sources to read; and choosing which resources will ultimately be used and cited in the research paper. Critical evaluation ranges from a series of mechanical techniques and strategies that can be applied to almost any information resource, to the more abstract and intuitive activities involved in using the knowledge you are acquiring about a topic to evaluate new information resources.

database   In the context of library research, a database can be any searchable online collection of citations to information resources or full-text information resources such as books or articles.

deep web   Also called the "invisible web," the deep web refers to content that cannot be found through traditional search engines such as Google. This happens either because the content is buried under too many layers of information on a particular web site or because the content is blocked from search engines (because it is fee-based or proprietary in some way).

depublishing   The practice of removing or altering electronic articles after publication.

directory   A reference book or online compilation listing people or organizations and providing contact information and brief facts.

ebook   A digital version of a book.

encyclopedia   A book or series of books or an online database containing short summary essays on topics. Encyclopedias can be broad or they can focus on a particular subject or discipline.

external consistency   An evaluation technique in which other information sources, primary or secondary, are used to corroborate what is stated in the source being evaluated.

fact-checking   A process used in editing and publishing in which facts are verified before a book, journal article, or other resource is published.

federated search engine   A library search engine that simultaneously searches many of the library-owned online databases and catalogs. Sometimes called broadcast searching or metasearching.

filter   A device used to narrow search results, usually to retrieve the most scholarly or relevant resources. Examples of filters include academic library online catalogs, scholarly article databases, or specific scholarly journals.

finding aid   A detailed description of the contents of a particular manuscript or archival collection that provides information about a specific item in the collection and how to locate that item.

footnotes   Raised Arabic numerals that follow the punctuation mark at the end of a sentence in a book, journal article, or research paper in the humanities, history, or legal studies. These numbered footnotes are then listed at the bottom of the relevant page or at the end of a paper, followed by a citation to the text being referenced.

free web   Information that is available for free on the web. Most online resources used by researchers are purchased by libraries and available to those affiliated with the library.

Freedom of Information Act   A law passed by Congress that provides a procedure for requesting government documents that have been classified.

free-text searching.   *See* **keyword searching**

gazetteer   A dictionary of geographic names that gives the location and brief information for each entry. Many gazetteers contain basic geographical features such as rivers, mountains, or cities located in a particular area.

government document   An information source produced by a government entity or with government funds.

hypothesis   An educated guess, a prediction, asked in the form of a question. A hypothesis attempts to predict the thesis of a research paper.

index   An alphabetical list of subjects and names found at the back of a book that provides page numbers or other types of locators leading to where the information can be found within the book. In the context of library research, indexes can also be defined as compilations in print or database form that provide subject, keyword, and author access to large quantities of citations. These citations lead the researcher to information resources such as articles or reports. Some indexes only include citations, some include abstracts, and some include links to full text.

institutional repository A digital collection created and compiled by a university or other institution in order to pull together the institutional knowledge and research, sometimes including scholarly articles, produced by that institution. These repositories are typically free to the public.

interlibrary loan An affiliated library user can borrow books and other materials not owned by his or her library from other libraries. The user fills out a form on the library web page requesting these resources.

internal consistency An evaluation technique that investigates whether the arguments made within a particular document are supported within the work itself or if there are contradictions put forward within the work itself.

"invisible college" A loosely defined unofficial network of scholars, all working on similar research questions, who become familiar with each other's research through conference attendance, shared research interests, publications, listservs, web pages, and other informal avenues.

journal A scholarly online or print publication that contains articles reporting on research. The articles are written by experts in a particular field. Most scholarly journals are carefully edited and use peer review to ensure that the research reported is of high quality. Journals are typically issued monthly or quarterly and most articles contain lengthy bibliographies citing other research.

keyword searching Keyword searching involves searching all of the available fields (such as author, title, subject heading, abstract, or in some cases full text) in an online catalog or database. Also called free-text searching. Keyword searching can sometimes be limited to specific fields (e.g., "keyword in title," when an exact title is not known).

legislative history The process of pulling together and analyzing all of the documents that led to a specific law being passed, from the introduction of the initial bill to the final passage of the law.

library online catalog The database that contains most of the books, journals, and other information resources owned by a specific library.

Library of Congress Subject Headings The controlled vocabulary created by catalogers and used by libraries since 1898 to assign subject headings to information resources. These subject headings are used in most academic library online catalogs to provide concise subject access to the materials owned by a specific library.

manuscripts Collections of personal unpublished papers and correspondence relating to or written by an individual.

microform Includes microfiche, microfilm, and microcard, early technology that allows vast amounts of materials to be preserved and collected in a smaller format for viewing on readers. Most microform readers can now print, and some are able to digitize materials onto a computer.

omission   An evaluation technique that involves determining if important information is left out of an information source. For example, a diary written at the time of the Civil War in the United States might be suspect if it failed to mention a major battle that took place in the same city in which the writer of the diary lived.

open access journal   A journal that is freely available over the web. The author or institution, rather than the publisher, retains copyright, and a commitment is made to make research available for free. Publishing costs are usually shifted from the reader to the author or institution producing the research.

oral history   A recorded conversation between an interviewer and subject about activities and incidents that have occurred in the past that were witnessed or in some way experienced by the subject. Oral histories allow researchers to interpret the past through the study of individual experiences.

paraphrase   Restating an author's words, usually using about the same number of words as the original author. *See also* **quotation, direct.**

parenthetical citation   Scientists and social scientists usually use parenthetical citations. The author and date are cited within the text—for example: (Lopez 1999)—with additional citation information provided at the end of the chapter, book, or article. Page numbers are sometimes included in the parenthetical citation.

peer review   A process in which a book or article is submitted by the prospective publisher to other experts to review and provide feedback to the original author. The identity of the author and the reviewers is sometimes kept confidential.

plagiarism   Copying the ideas or language of another writer without formally acknowledging that writer through the use of a citation to the work.

preprint publication   An article that is available prior to publication in order to share knowledge quickly about a topic. This type of publication is especially common in the sciences. Preprints can be found at preprint archives or servers.

primary source   A document that contains information written by the observer of an event or one of the first people to record an event after it occurred.

proximity searching   Proximity searching refers to a number of techniques used in online databases to indicate that words should appear next to each other, within a certain number of words of each other, and/or in a certain order. Proximity operators are not standardized, though many databases use quotation marks to search phrases.

quotation, direct   The writing down of another author's words exactly as they appear in the author's text. Involves using quotation marks or indenting the words, and using a footnote or endnote to indicate the original text in which the author's words appeared.

reference book   A book in print or electronic form that is used to look up facts, concise authoritative summaries, or overviews about an issue or topic.

researcher bias The ideas and value systems brought to the research being conducted by the person doing the research.

review article A scholarly journal article that provides a systematic review and critique of the research on a particular topic. These articles are valuable for the researcher because they point out the weaknesses in earlier research, indicate areas where more research is needed, and pull together a list of the most important articles that have been written about a specific topic.

scholarly book Also called a monograph, this is a book that is written by a professor or other expert in order to analyze, review, and further the state of knowledge about a subject. These books usually contain extensive bibliographies that connect a scholar's work to earlier research by other scholars. They are published by scholarly rather than commercial publishers.

secondary source A book, article, or other information resource that reports on, analyzes, summarizes, or distills in some way information garnered from primary sources.

serendipity Often mentioned by scholars with regard to research, serendipity can occur when browsing the book stacks or online library catalog. While retrieving one book on a particular topic, the eye falls on a related topic or book and suddenly new creative connections are made about a research problem.

special collections Archival, manuscript, or rare book collections are kept in this restricted area of a library. The special collections area of the library usually provides carefully restricted access to these valuable materials.

stare decisis All case law is based on the doctrine of *stare decisis*, Latin for "to stand by that which is decided." The U.S. legal system relies on past legal decisions—past *precedent*—to decide current cases.

style manual A print or online book that indicates exactly how to format the citations that are listed in the references section at the end of a research paper or published work. Style manuals also provide information about other aspects of the writing process.

subject encyclopedia A subject encyclopedia provides a concise overview of the current state of research on a particular topic. Unlike a general encyclopedia, such as *Encyclopedia Britannica*, subject encyclopedias focus on one broad subject. They are valuable because they provide a concise overview of research findings on topics related to their subject area, and a list of the key books and articles on particular topics.

subject heading A subject heading is a precise term assigned to a database record that describes the subject or content of a work. The term is selected from a controlled vocabulary list such as the Library of Congress Subject Headings, which is used to describe the contents of library online catalogs.

thesis statement A general statement in a research paper or article that presents the conclusions of the research. The paper provides the support for the conclusion stated in the thesis.

time and place A rule used by historians to evaluate the quality of a primary source. The closer in time and place a source and its creator were to an event, the better validity the source may have. A firsthand observer who witnessed a Civil War battle and wrote a letter about it will have more worth as a primary source than an account written by someone who was not a witness and relied on accounts from others, or who wrote about the event long after it occurred.

trade book   A book published by a commercial publisher that is sold to the general public. Sometimes trade books report on information that originated in more scholarly works. Trade books are written in a less formal or technical way and are easier to read than scholarly books.

truncation   Used in database and online catalog searching to capture different word endings or alternative spellings. A symbol such as "*" is used as in the following example: Therap*. This search will retrieve "therapy," therapeutic," and "therapeutical."

weblog   *See* **blog**

wiki   A collaborative web site comprised of the collective work of many authors. Wikis, named after the Hawaiian word "wikiwiki," meaning "quick," are simple to use and edit. There is frequently no review of pages that are edited, and many wikis are open to the general public, usually without any registration procedures. Wikis are popular with scientists and software engineers, but they are starting to be used by other people who are collaborating on projects. Wikis vary tremendously in their authoritativeness and reliability.

yearbook   An annual compendium of facts, statistics, and sometimes photographs pertaining to events in the previous year relating to a particular country, subject, or discipline.

REFERENCES

Commission on Colleges, Southern Association of Colleges and Schools (SACS). 1996. *Criteria for accreditation*, section 5.1.2 [Library and Other Information Resources]. 10th ed. (December).

Shapiro, Jeremy J., and Shelley K. Hughes. 1996. Information literacy as a liberal art: Enlightenment proposals for a new curriculum. *Educom Review* 31, no. 2 (March/April). http://www.educause.edu/pub/er/review/reviewarticles/31231.html. Accessed March 3, 2005.

Title Index

Subject Index

Titles of books and web resources mentioned in the text are indexed in the Title Index. Titles of journal databases are listed in the Appendix.

About the Author

LESLIE F. STEBBINS coordinates the Library Intensive Program at Brandeis University Libraries. She also serves as a liaison to the Brandeis University Sociology Department, Politics Department, Women's Study Program, and the Heller School for Social Policy and Management. Her previous works include *Work and Family in America: A Reference Handbook* and *Women and Equality in the Workplace* (co-authored with Dr. Janet Giele).